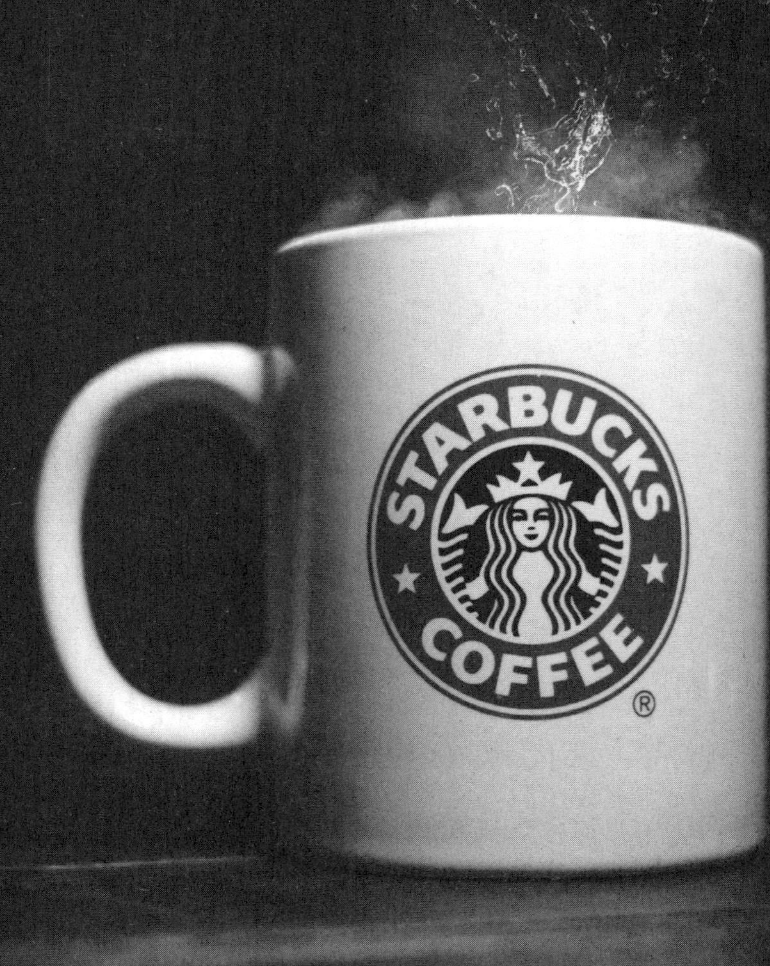
STARBUCKS
COFFEE

STARBUCKS

CREATIVE COMPANIES

PAMELA DELL AND SARA GILBERT

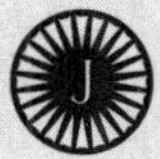

JAICO PUBLISHING HOUSE

Ahmedabad Bangalore Chennai
Delhi Hyderabad Kolkata Mumbai

Published by Jaico Publishing House
A-2 Jash Chambers, 7-A Sir Phirozshah Mehta Road
Fort, Mumbai - 400 001
jaicopub@jaicobooks.com
www.jaicobooks.com

Published in arrangement with
The Creative Company
2140 Howard Drive West,
North Mankato, MN 56003, USA

To be sold only in India, Bangladesh, Bhutan,
Pakistan, Nepal, Sri Lanka and the Maldives.

Design by Graham Morgan
Art direction by Tom Morgan
Edited by Jill Kalz

Images by Alamy (foodfolio, john angerson, Lee Frost),
Getty (Justin Sullivan, Patricia Monteiro/Bloomberg,
Peter Adams, Suzanne Opton), Pexels (Alesya
Gorbunova), Erik Mclean, Viktoria Alipatova),
Unsplash (Anton Ponomarenko,
Asael Peña, Crystal Jo,
Deepak Raj, Gregory Hayes,
Hamza Inayat, Herry Sutanto,
Jiawei Zhao, Julia Solonina,
June Andrei George, Roméo
A., Timothy Eberly),
Wikimedia Commons (Another Believer, Backupboy,
elliotstoller, KKPCW, Postdlf, While editing)

STARBUCKS
ISBN 978-93-48098-39-9

First Jaico Impression: 2025

Printed by
Parksons Graphics Pvt. Ltd., Mumbai

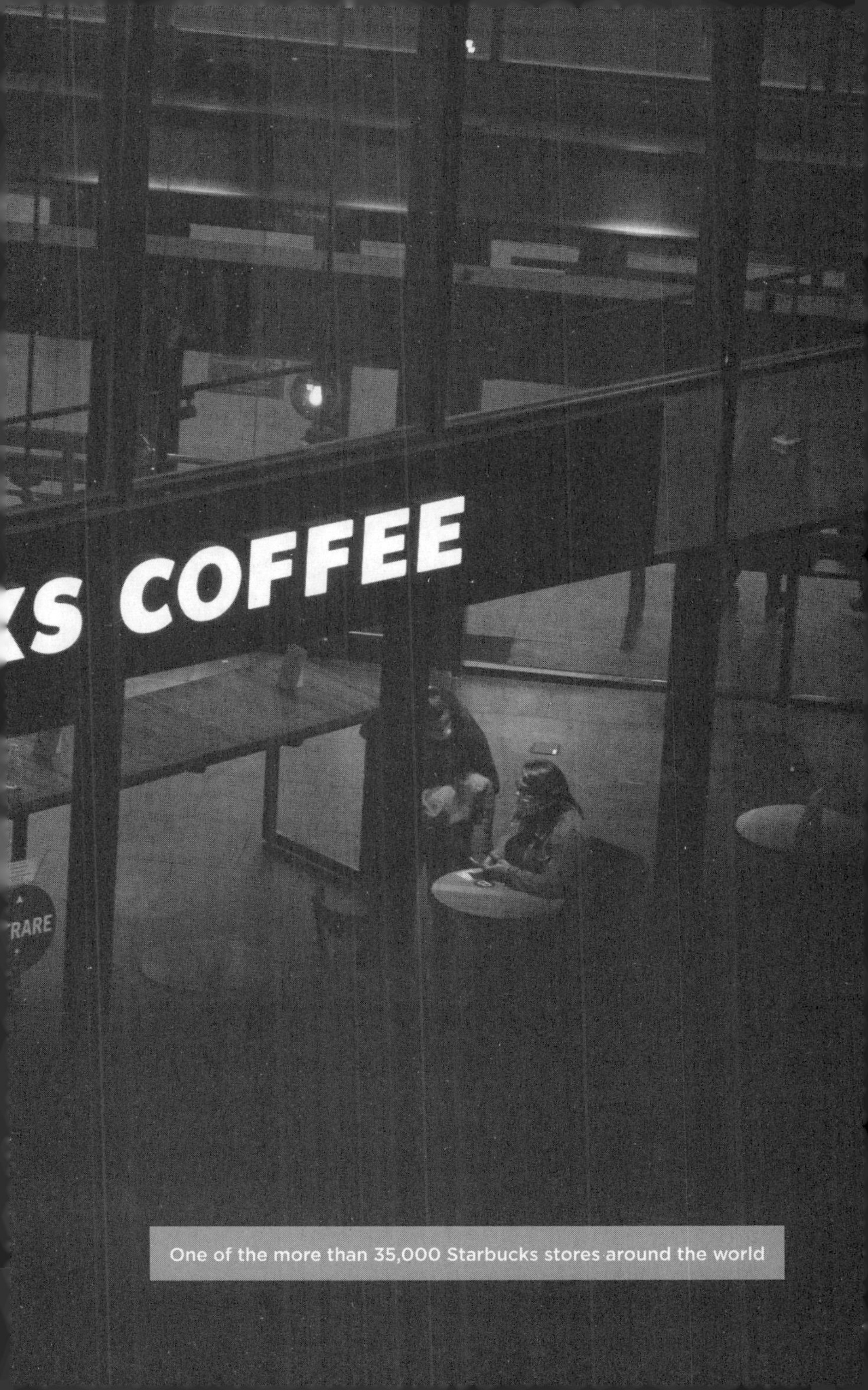

One of the more than 35,000 Starbucks stores around the world

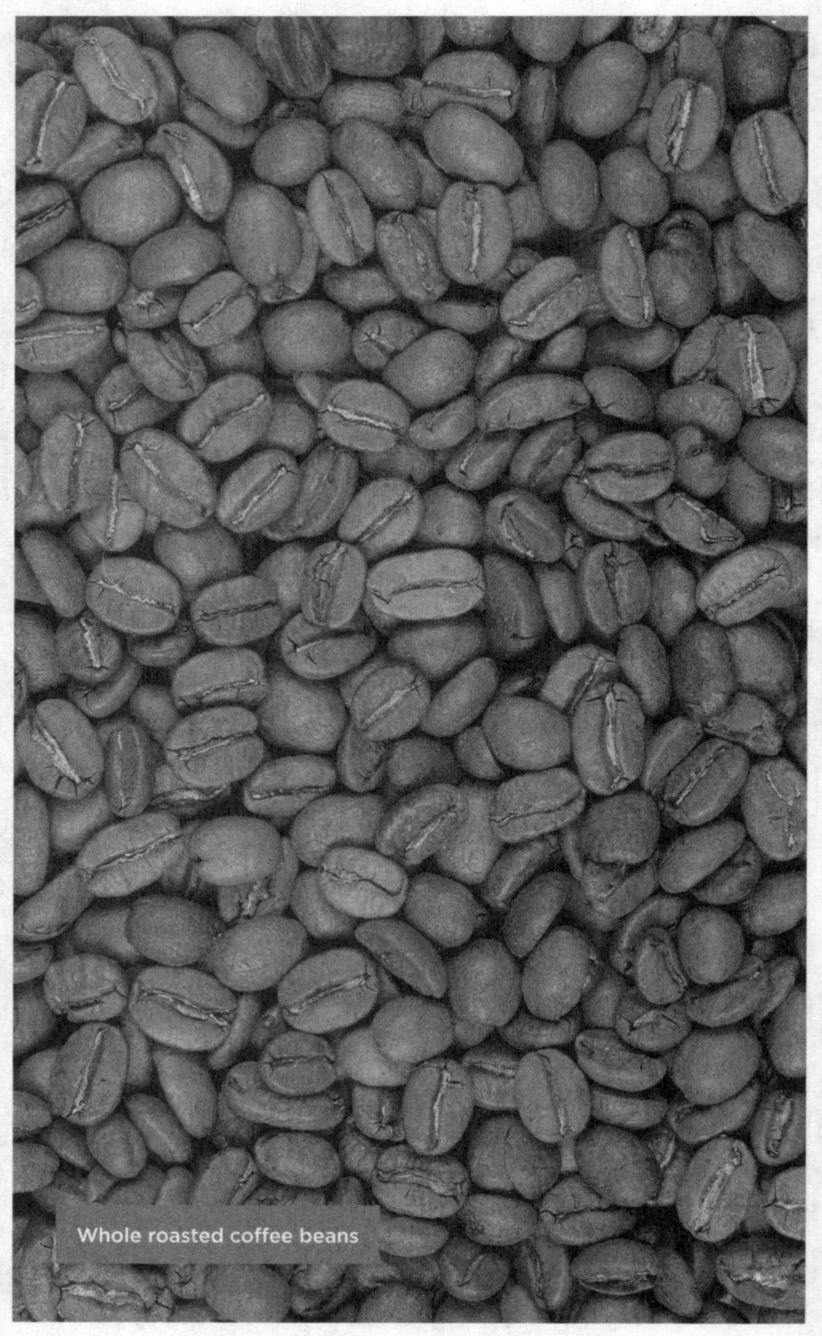

Whole roasted coffee beans

CONTENTS

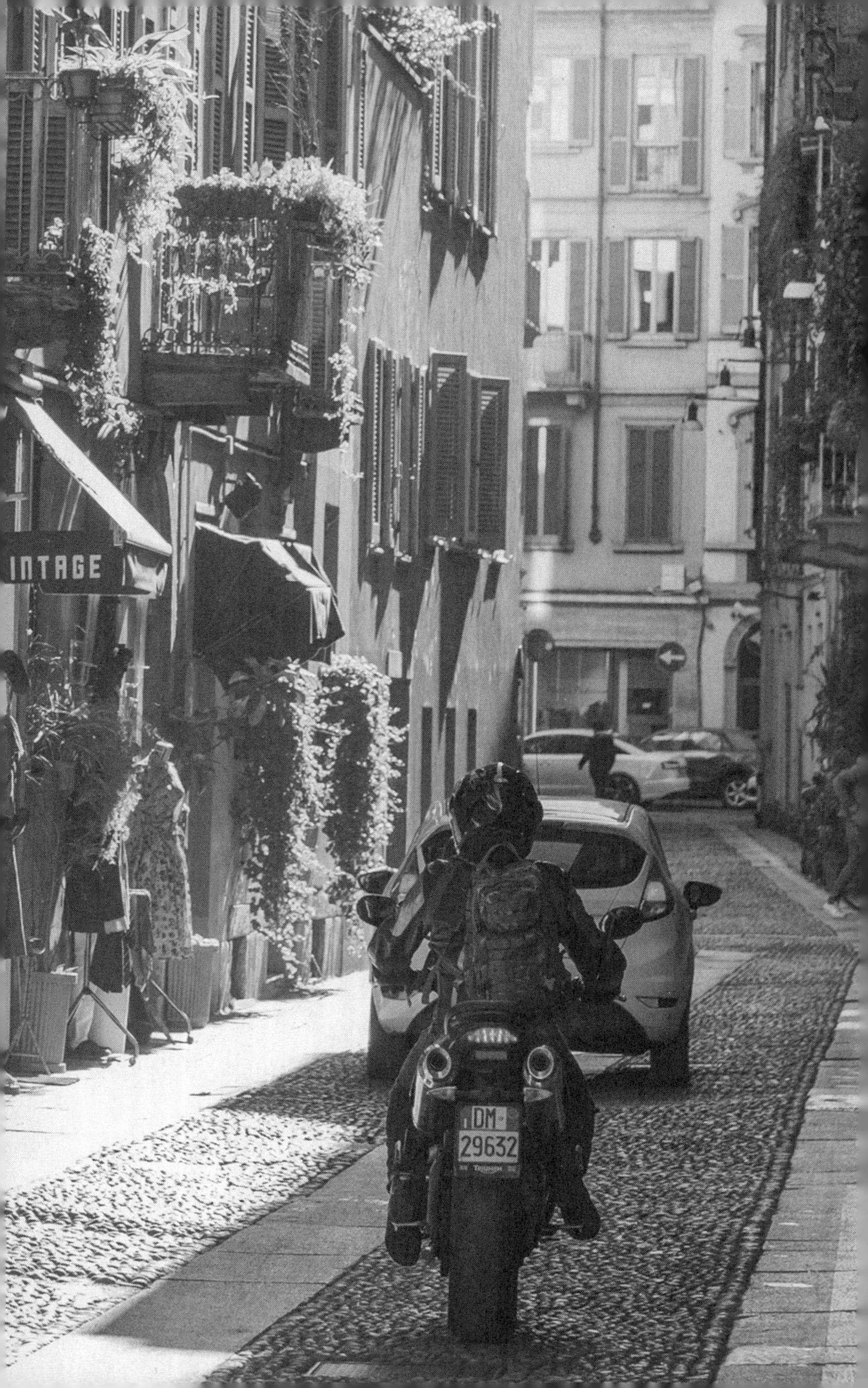
INTAGE
DM
29632

Introduction

The bustling, modern city of Milan is Italy's northern hub of business and industry. Long known for its sophisticated fashion and design, it's also a magnet for tourists who come to view centuries-old artworks and walk through medieval castles. On a lesser scale, but still culturally significant, Milan is home to about 1,500 social-gathering spots known as coffee bars or coffeehouses.

OPPOSITE: Buildings line the narrow streets of Milan, Italy, with shops at ground level and apartments above.

In 1983, a 30-year-old American man had an awakening of sorts in this vibrant city. You might say he "woke up and smelled the coffee."

While in Milan on business, New Yorker Howard Schultz was immediately drawn to the coffee bars. He was struck by their relaxed, welcoming atmosphere. The warm, rich smell of roasting coffee hung in the air. Customers chatted in a familiar, first-name way with the **baristas** who made their coffees to order. They ate warm pastries and drank

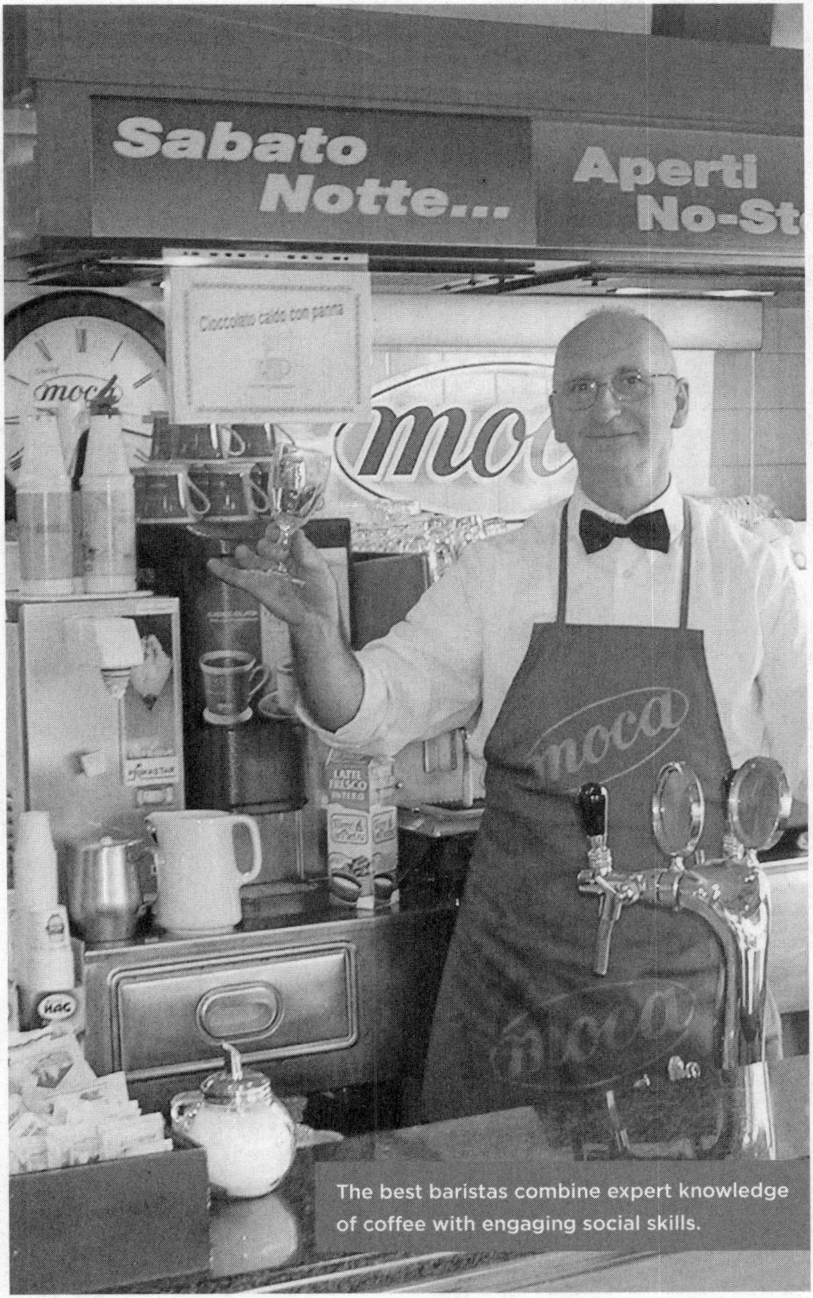

The best baristas combine expert knowledge of coffee with engaging social skills.

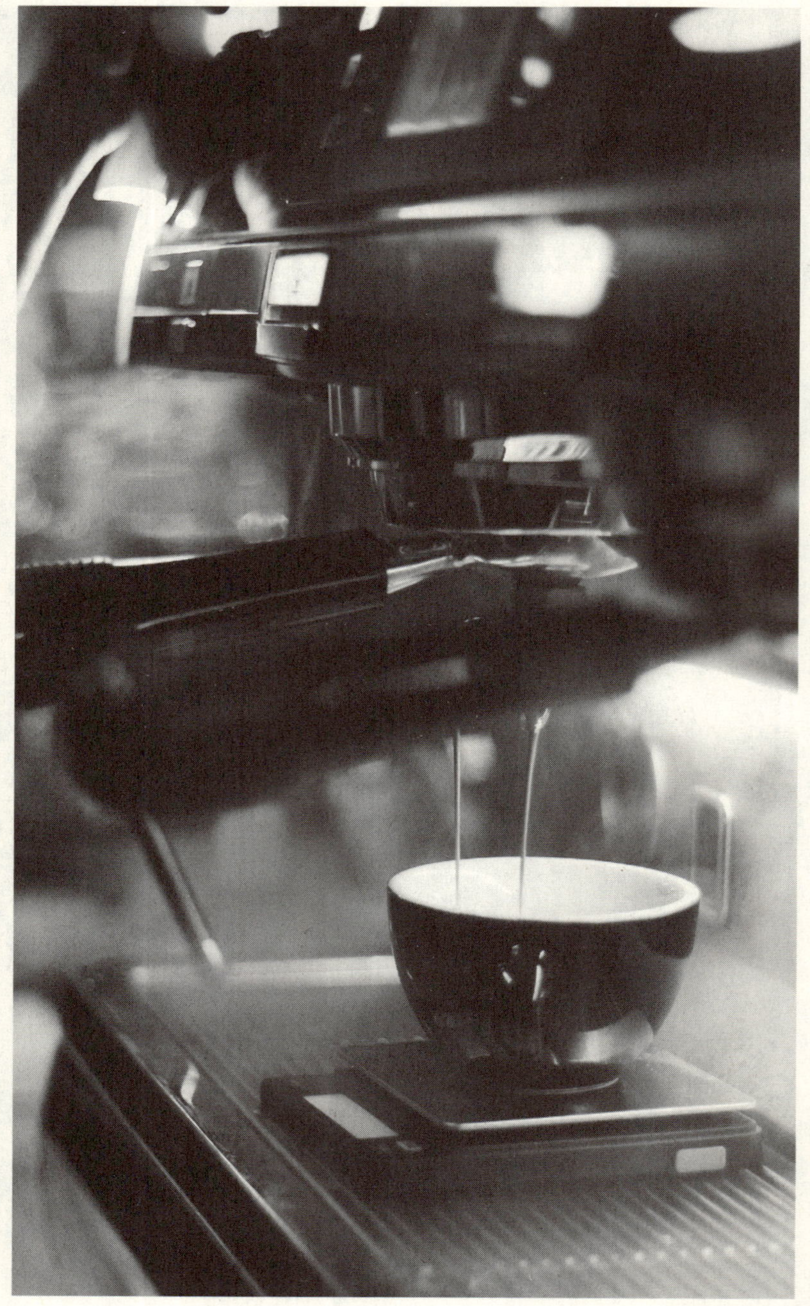

OPPOSITE An espresso machine forces a tiny amount of hot water through tightly packed, ground coffee beans.

strong **espresso**. And these places were lively at all hours.

The laid-back coffee bar scene, common throughout Italy, struck a chord with Schultz. Back in the states, most people simply bought ground coffee in tins at the supermarket and boiled it at home. But in Italy, coffee-drinking was a cultural ritual. By the time he returned to the United States, Schultz was a man on fire—and a small, regional company called Starbucks was headed straight for the big time.

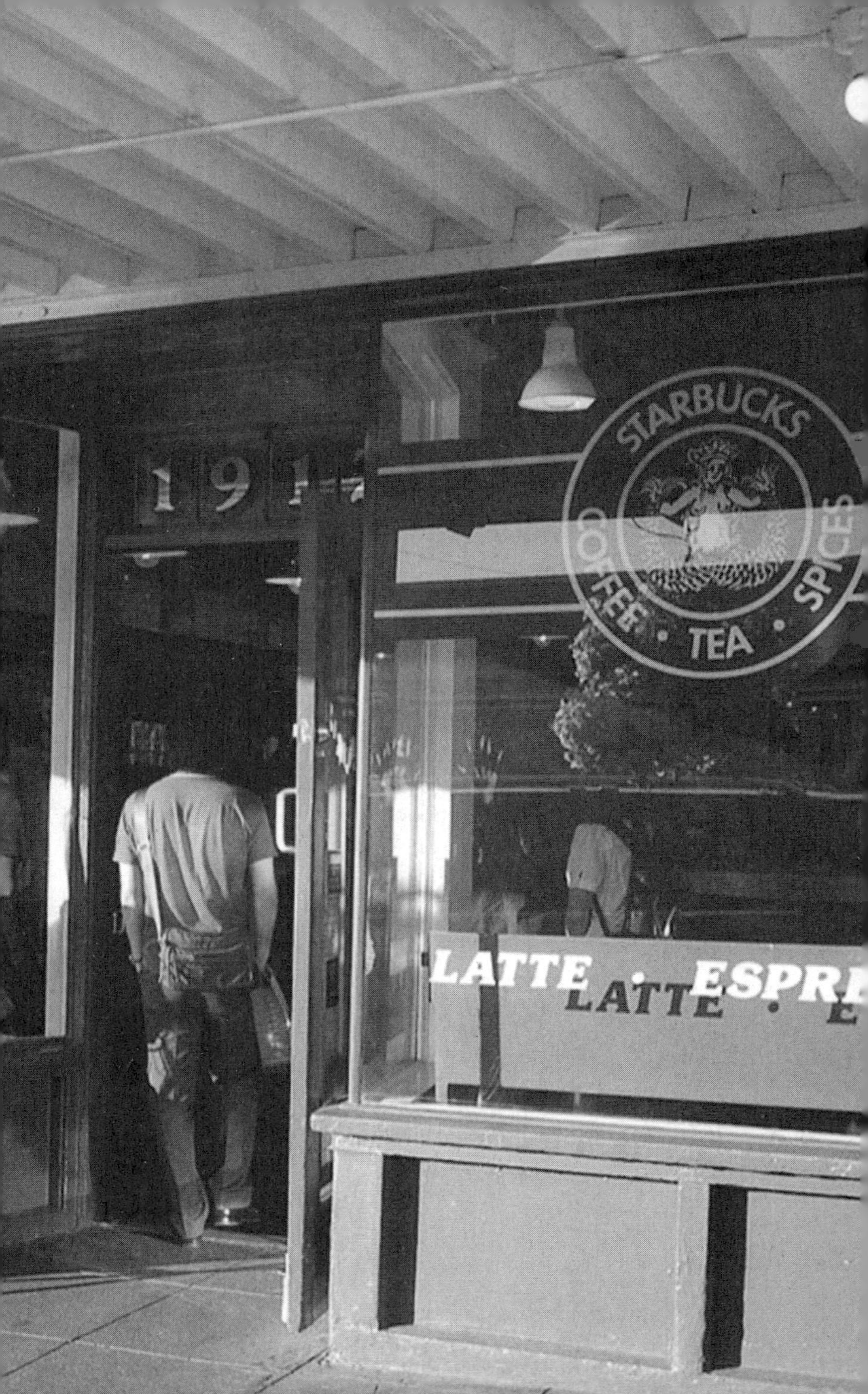
STARBUCKS
COFFEE • TEA • SPICES
LATTE

In the Beginning

It all started with three young men who bonded through complementary skills and shared dreams of success. Jerry Baldwin, Gordon Bowker, and Zev Siegl had met in 1962, when they were all just 20 years old. Some years later, gainfully employed in Seattle, Washington, the three friends still mused over going into business together. They tried partnering up in different creative ways, but nothing stuck.

OPPOSITE: Although not officially the first Starbucks to open, the store in Seattle's Pike Place Market is today refered to as the original.

Finally, Bowker sprung an idea with realistic potential. He'd been driving all the way from Seattle to Vancouver, British Columbia (about a 2.5-hour drive, one way), just to buy fresh-roasted coffee from a company there. He purchased roasted coffee beans for himself and for friends who wanted that same rich coffee experience not found in nearby stores or restaurants. *What about opening a coffee business of their own in Seattle?* Bowker thought. Instead of driving 140 miles (225 kilometers) to purchase beans, they could enjoy—and sell—quality fresh-roasted coffee without going anywhere. Baldwin and Siegl were up for giving it a go.

A lot of planning, hard work, and research followed. The men also had to come up with the necessary funds to start a business. At last, on March

30, 1971, Starbucks Coffee Tea and Spice Company opened its doors for the first time. Customers could buy coffee, tea, teapots, spices, coffeemakers, and coffee grinders.

Siegl had done his research well. The partners ultimately chose to buy their whole roasted coffee beans from Peet's Coffee. The well-established company in Berkeley, California, was the best in the business. Baldwin, Bowker, and Siegl soon learned the entire roasting process from Peet's founder himself, Netherlands native Alfred Peet. That knowledge allowed them to later buy raw beans directly from suppliers. "There was no one in his league," Siegl recalled about Peet.

After opening day, the young company grew gradually. A couple more stores opened, one in Seattle's University Village shopping center and the other in the city of Edmonds, north of Seattle. Starbucks's fortunes rose and fell over the next few years as worldwide coffee bean prices rose and fell. There were some close calls, but **investors** stepped in to help keep the company alive. Things stabilized—until the three partners received notice that the building that housed their first store was scheduled for a tear-down. It wasn't good news. But in 1977, Starbucks reopened in the famous Pike Place Market, an even better location than the first. The Pike Place "original" Starbucks has been there ever since and is now a tourist attraction.

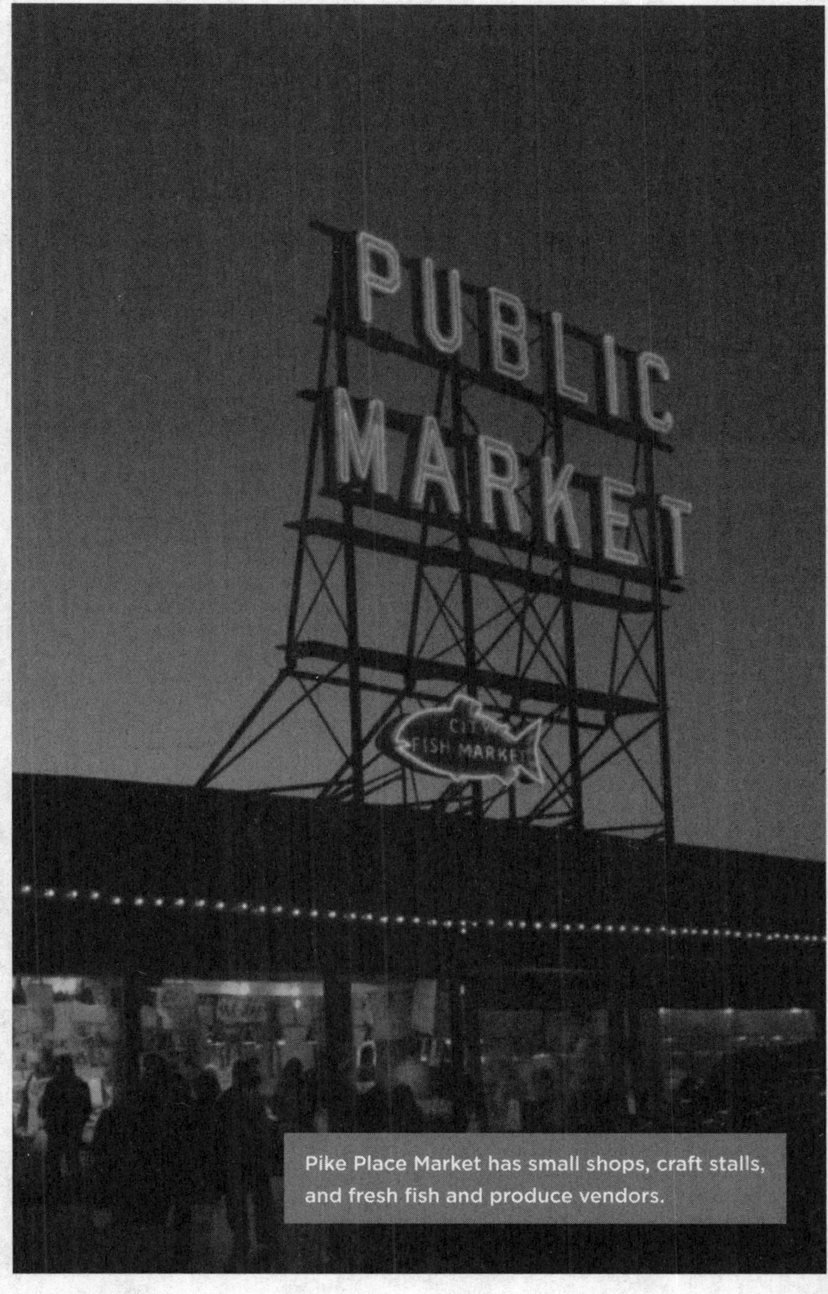

Pike Place Market has small shops, craft stalls, and fresh fish and produce vendors.

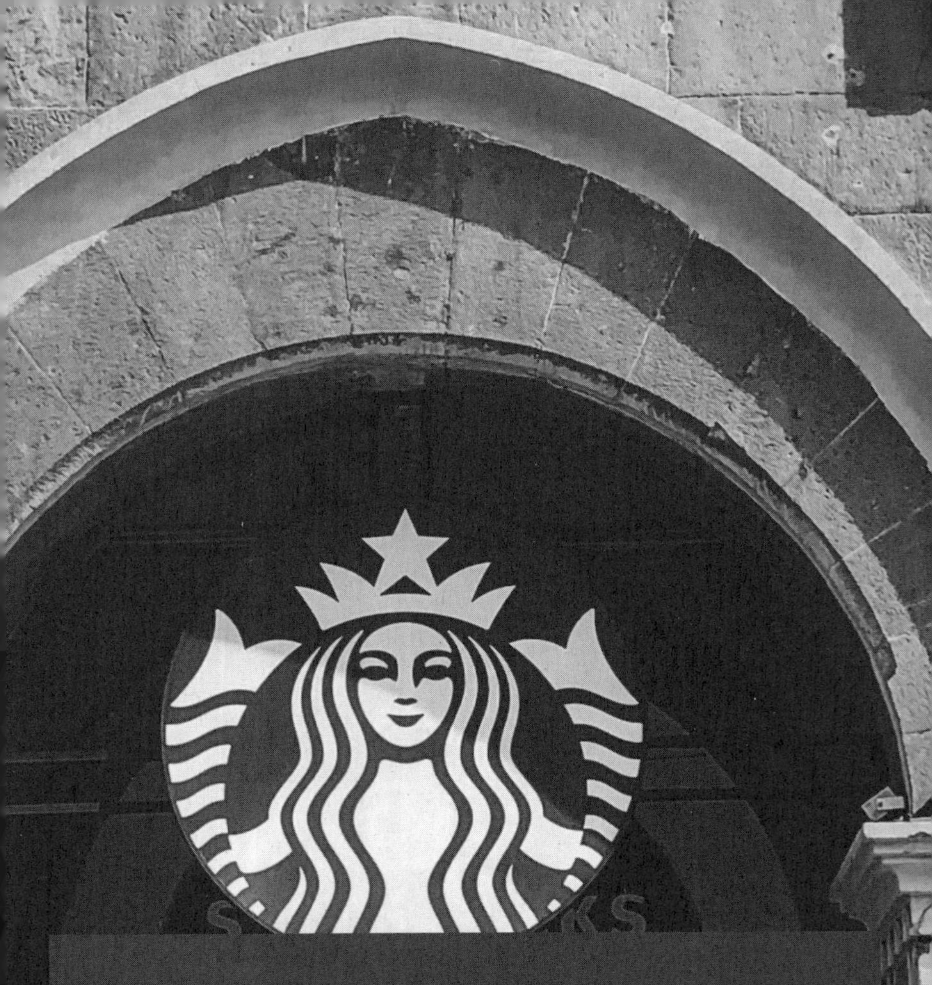

What's in a Name?

The Starbucks name was the inspiration of Gordon Bowker. Looking at an old mining map that hung in the waterfront office of his then business, Bowker saw a curious town name: Starbo. He immediately associated that with Starbuck, the first mate on the whaling ship *Pequod* in Herman Melville's novel *Moby Dick*. "From that moment, it became Starbucks," Bowker said, about naming the new coffee company. "I didn't really have to convince Zev [Siegl] and Jerry [Baldwin] very hard." As for the twin-tailed mermaid, she's based on the seagoing creatures from Greek mythology called sirens. The sirens' singing lured unwitting sailors to their doom.

By 1980, after nearly 10 years in business, Starbucks was on solid ground. The founders had multiple stores in and around Seattle, all doing a brisk trade. They were selling their fresh-roasted coffee to hundreds of restaurants and **wholesale** companies. Starbucks was dominating the coffee market in the Pacific Northwest. The business was all the founders had hoped it would be. But change was coming.

In 1981, an ambitious young man from New York City walked into Starbucks, curious about the company. That man was Howard Schultz. At the time, Schultz worked for Hammerplast, a Swedish firm that sold European coffee-brewing equipment and other related merchandise. Starbucks had been buying in large quantities. As Hammerplast's director of sales, Schultz wanted to see the reason for this himself.

That West Coast visit sparked Schultz's imagination. Siegl had left Starbucks in 1980, interested in developing new start-up businesses. But Bowker and Baldwin were still going strong. Both were as passionate as ever about selling high-grade coffee. They were still equally committed to passing their knowledge on to their staff and customers. Their enthusiasm was contagious. Schultz returned to New York thinking, *What a great company. What a great city. I'd love to be part of that.*

Unfortunately for Schultz, it was not to be. At least not right away. Schultz pleaded his case to Bowker and Baldwin, hoping they'd hire him to do **marketing**. He met with them in person a second time the following year. Stubbornly determined, he made follow-up calls after they turned him down. Finally, in the fall of 1982, Schultz's persistence paid off. The Starbucks founders gave in and hired him as director of retail operations and marketing.

The next year, 1983, was a fateful one for Starbucks. That was the year the company sent Schultz on the eye-opening business trip to Milan.

Starbucks had been offering coffee to its customers from the very beginning. They gave shoppers tasting samples of the brews sold in the stores, helping them decide what to purchase. In 1982, before Schultz was hired, the company had begun

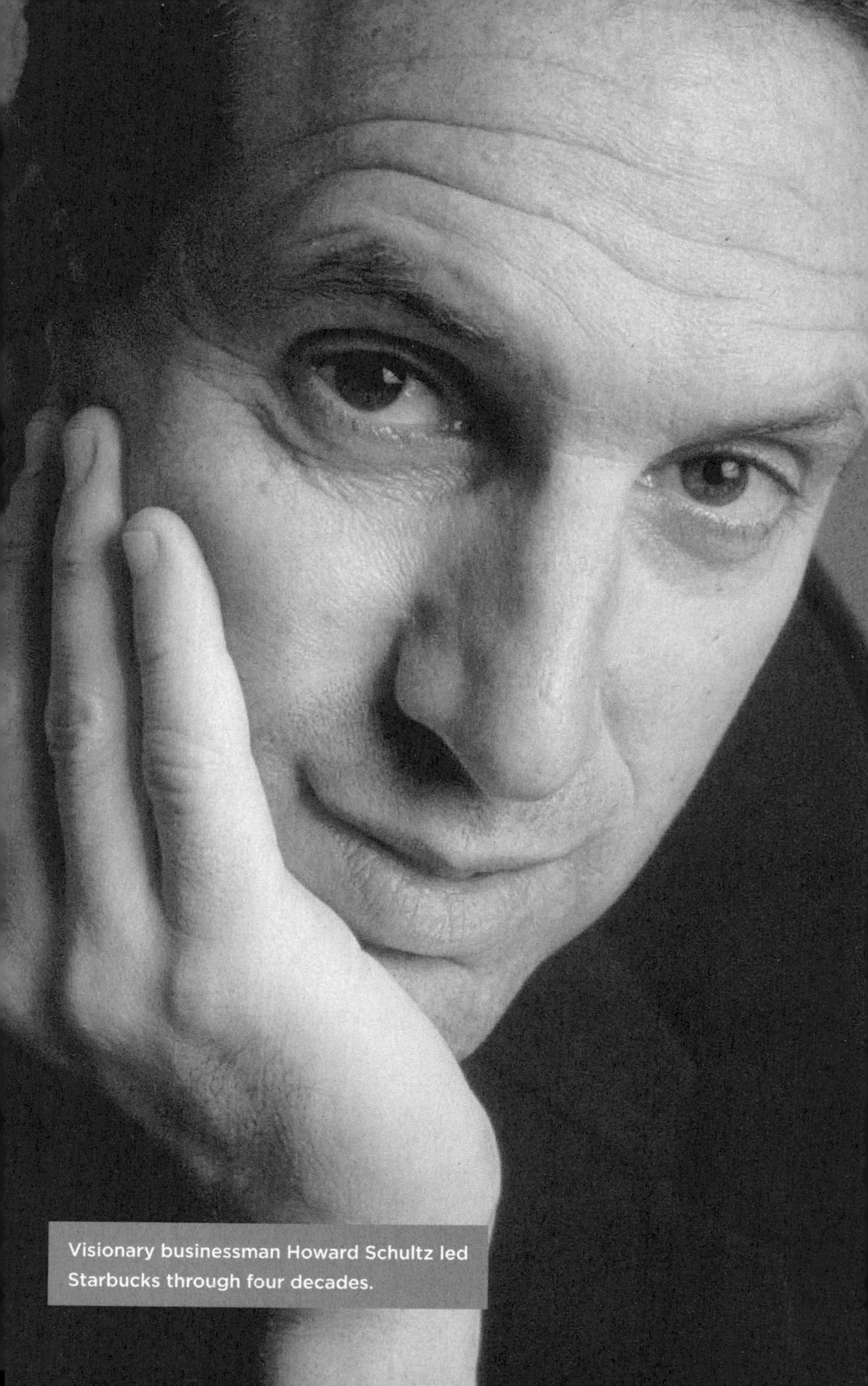

Visionary businessman Howard Schultz led Starbucks through four decades.

casually selling cups of coffee at the University Way store. But Bowker and Baldwin weren't interested in taking that concept further. Based on what they'd learned about Peet's in Berkeley, they didn't see individual coffee sales as adding much **profit** to the company. They didn't think it was worth their time. Their focus was on what they'd always done best—roasting and selling premium packaged coffee beans.

But once Schultz returned from Italy, he began his second campaign to change things up at Starbucks. He had seen so clearly the sense

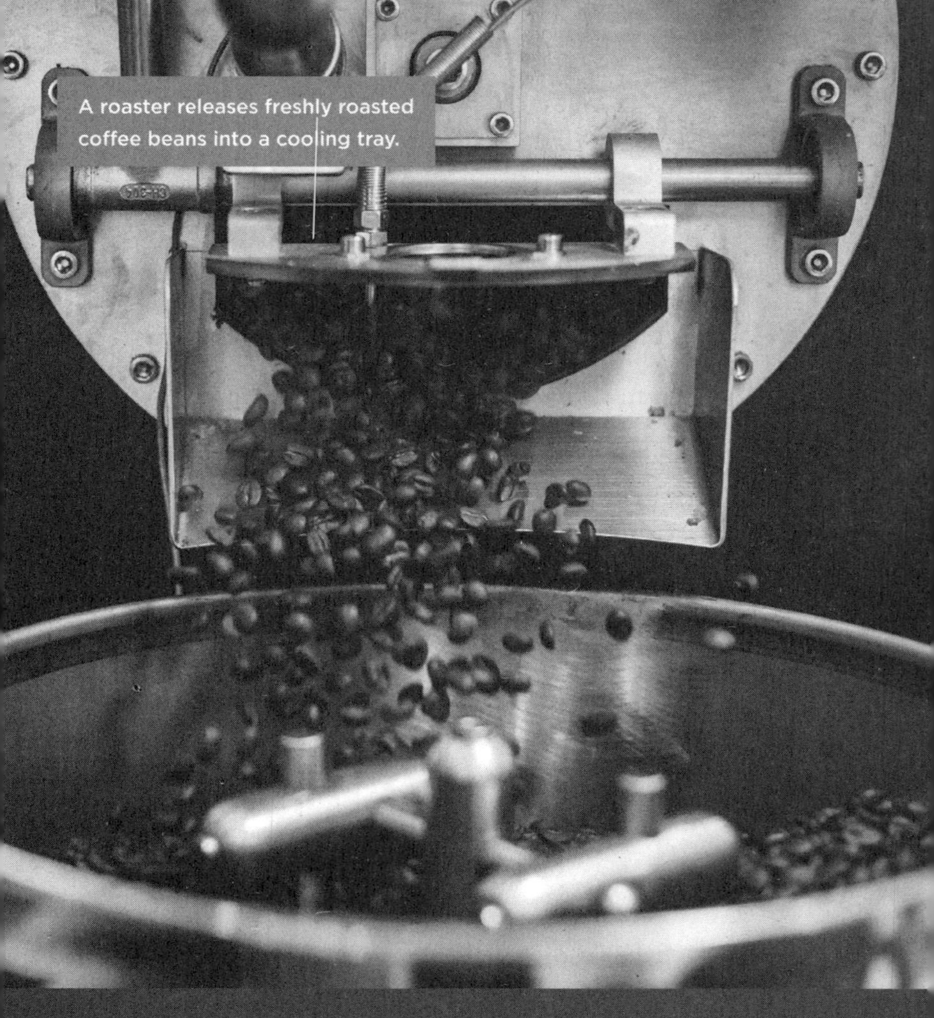

A roaster releases freshly roasted coffee beans into a cooling tray.

The Art of Roasting

Roasting green coffee beans to perfection is an art. When Starbucks was getting its start, Jerry Baldwin wanted to learn that art from the best. His research led him to Alfred Peet, who had opened his coffee business in Berkeley, California, in 1966. Peet's rich, deep-roasted coffee was an American first. His first store soon became known as the "caffeine Mecca of the West Coast." In 1971, Peet began selling beans to the Starbucks founders and agreed to teach Baldwin how to roast his own. Without Peet's, there never would have been a Starbucks.

of community and loyalty the Milan coffee houses generated. He envisioned Starbucks as the ideal company to recreate that same social atmosphere—not just in the Seattle area but across the United States.

Once again, Bowker and Baldwin resisted. They were in business to sell beans and a few other products, they told Schultz. Not only that, they had several other business ventures demanding their time. This made them reluctant to expand Starbucks or to adopt any new business models. But Schultz was a persistent, driven man. A man with a bigger vision. From that point on, things would never be the same for Starbucks. The big fish in a small pond was destined to take over the entire ocean.

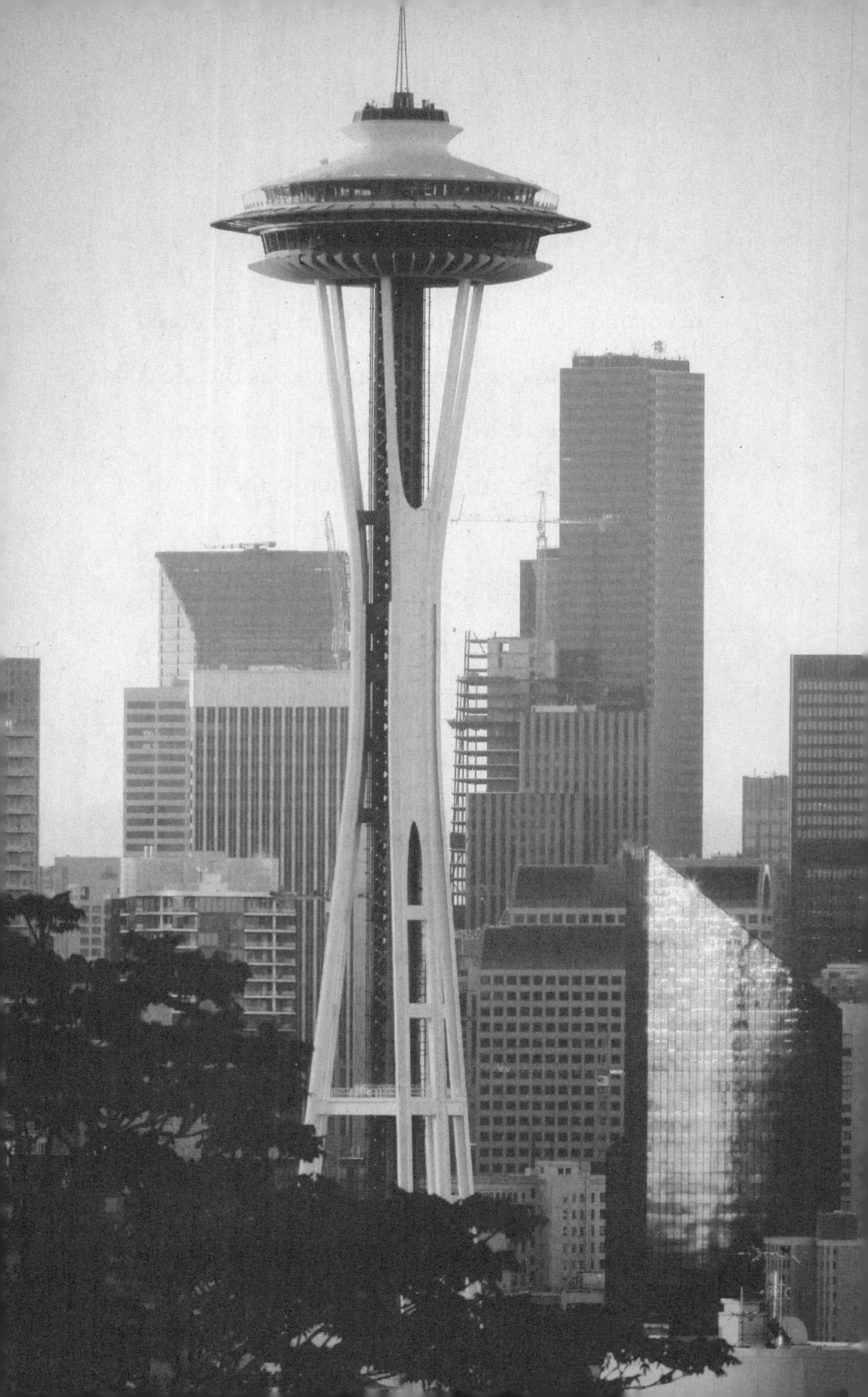

Taking Over

In May 1984, a new Starbucks opened in downtown Seattle, giving Howard Schultz a tiny taste of success. He convinced Gordon Bowker and Jerry Baldwin to try out a small espresso bar there. On the bar's first day, the store served about 400 coffees, including the first-ever Starbucks Caffé Lattes.

OPPOSITE: The iconic observation tower called the Space Needle overlooks downtown Seattle, a city of more than 750,000 people.

Within a couple months, Starbucks sales had doubled. The store had lines out the door. Inside, baristas worked as fast as they could to fill orders.

If anything indicated what a success the espresso bars could be, it was the sales numbers. Nevertheless, that kind of future still didn't interest either owner. Burning with a futuristic vision of taking Starbucks to the next level, Schultz was frustrated. When he realized he would never get anywhere with Bowker and Baldwin, he took a giant leap of faith.

In 1985, Schultz gave notice that he was leaving Starbucks to pursue his dream. Because he still felt loyal to the company, however, it was a difficult decision. Baldwin made it easier. Believing in what Schultz wanted to do, Baldwin gave him $150,000 in **seed money**, becoming Schultz's first investor. Schultz's initial plan involved opening eight Italian-style coffee bars in and around Seattle. But $150,000 wasn't enough to launch even one. It took a while, but once he managed to raise all the money he needed, Schultz opened his first Il Giornale [eel jhor-NAH-lay]. In English, the words mean "the newspaper." The coffee bar's name came from one of Milan's daily papers.

Schultz's first store opened in downtown Seattle in April 1986 and did big business right from the start. Whether served plain, as a shot of espresso, or with steamed milk, the coffee didn't disappoint. Schultz bought his roasted beans from Starbucks.

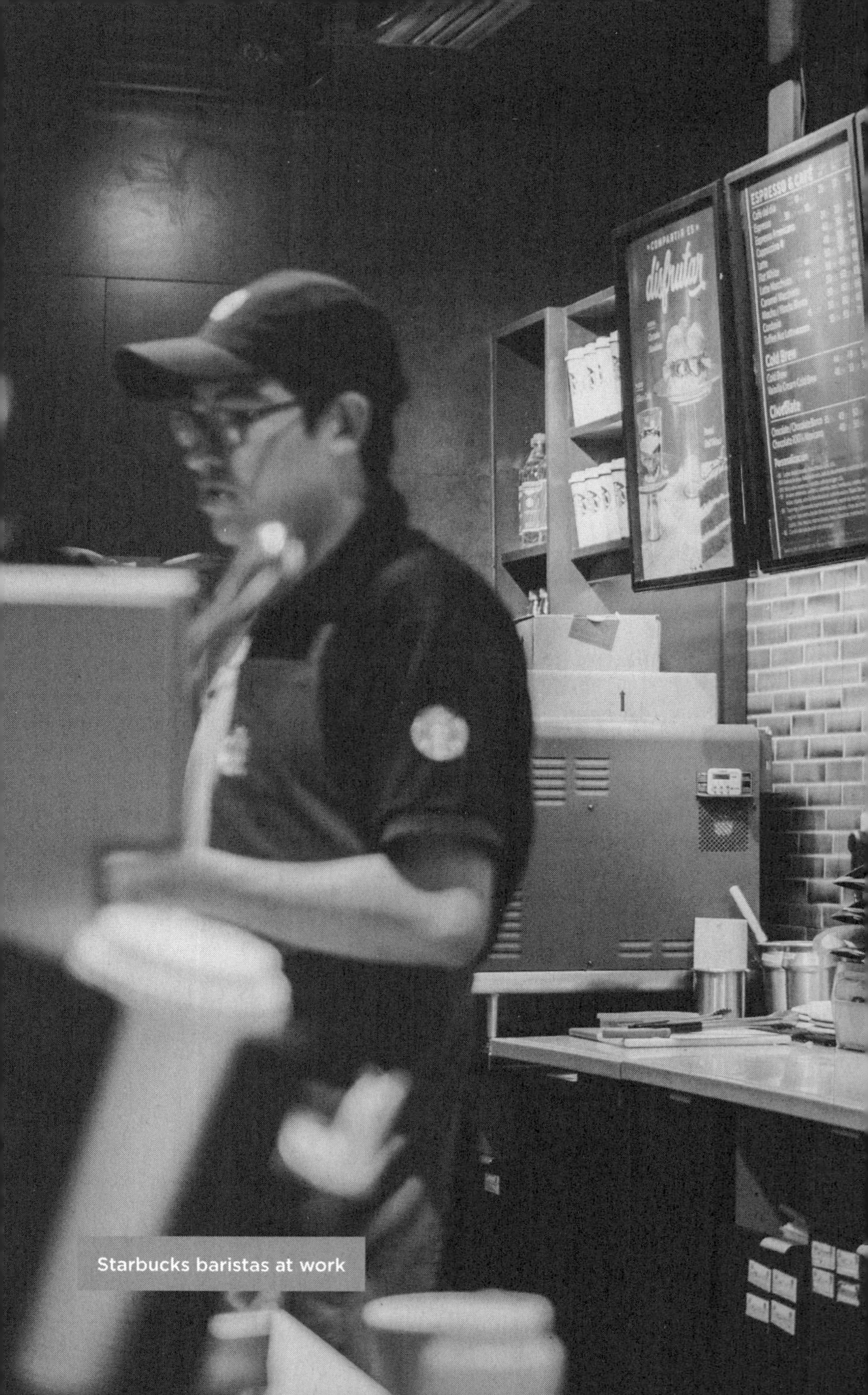

Starbucks baristas at work

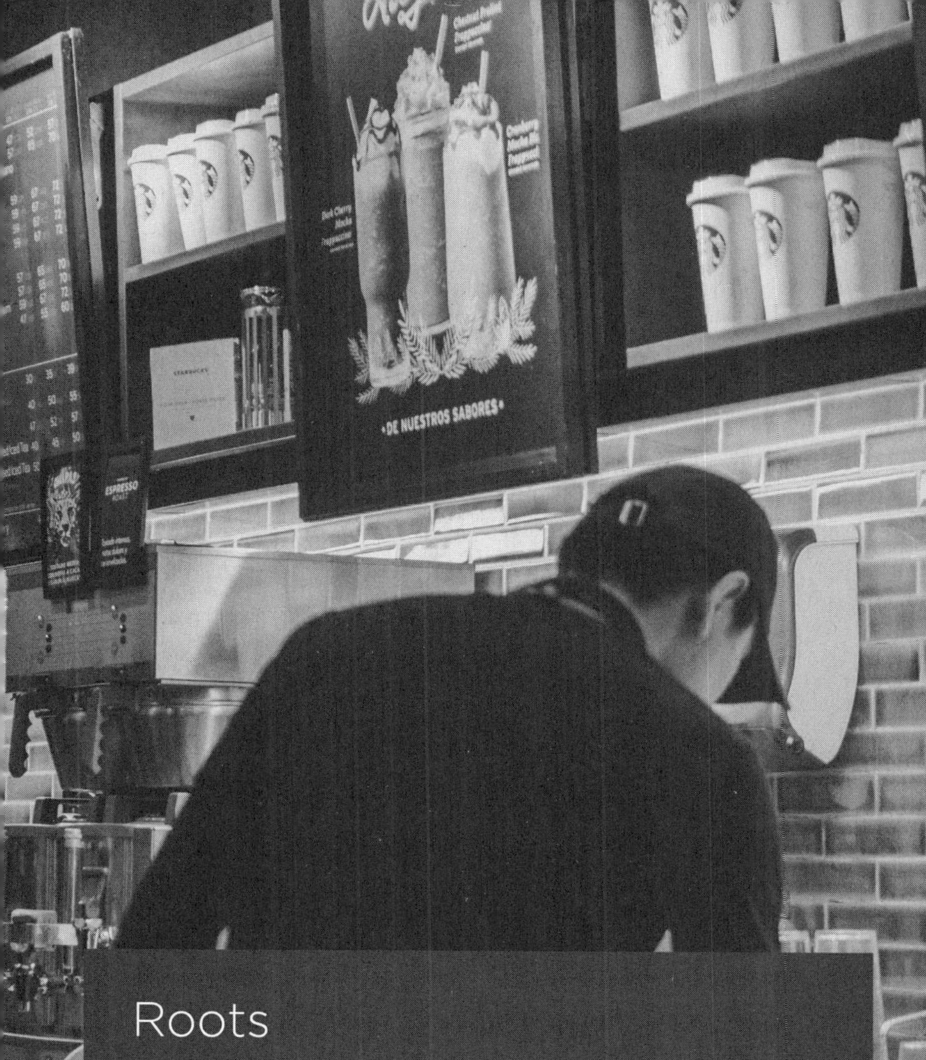

Roots

Howard Schultz grew up in a Brooklyn, New York, low-rent housing project. His father had moved from job to job, barely making enough money to keep his wife and two children housed, fed, and clothed. Schultz believed his dad had been a hard worker who was disrespected and beaten down by "the system." Having witnessed his father's struggles, Schultz vowed to give his own employees more advantages in return for their hard work. The Starbucks CEO prides himself on having "built the kind of company that my father never got a chance to work for."

In slightly more than one year, Il Giornale was operating in three locations. A second store had opened in Seattle and a third in Vancouver, British Columbia. Annual sales reached nearly $500,000 in 1987. Schultz was on target to expand his Il Giornale business even further. However, he got some big, unexpected news that changed everything: Starbucks was for sale.

Bowker and Baldwin had mutually decided to give up Starbucks to pursue their other business interests. They offered Schultz a limited-time, exclusive offer. They would give him a chance to raise the money to meet their $3.8 million asking price before they considered any other offers.

In the mid-1980s, high-grade coffee was mostly foreign to Americans. There was nothing fresh about grocery-store-bought ground coffee. In fact, U.S.

coffee consumption was decreasing. Knowing this, some potential investors didn't believe the public would pay a high price for a cup of coffee when they could get one for 50 cents or so. But again, Schultz was determined. Before long, he had managed to find investors willing to take a risk on a passionate young man with a big dream.

On August 15, 1987, Schultz walked out of an office building and into one of his Il Giornale coffee bars across the street. He was burning to get going on the plan he'd had since his first trip to Milan. Now, nothing was stopping him. In that office building, he had just successfully closed the Starbucks deal. As the new owner of the company, he saw the future as limitless. Schultz meant to introduce the whole world to a coffee culture in its best sense. He would start an entire new chapter in the Starbucks success playbook.

At that point, Starbucks had more stores than Il Giornale did. It also had an excellent reputation in the Seattle area, whereas Il Gironale was new and barely known. So, it only made sense to merge the two companies under

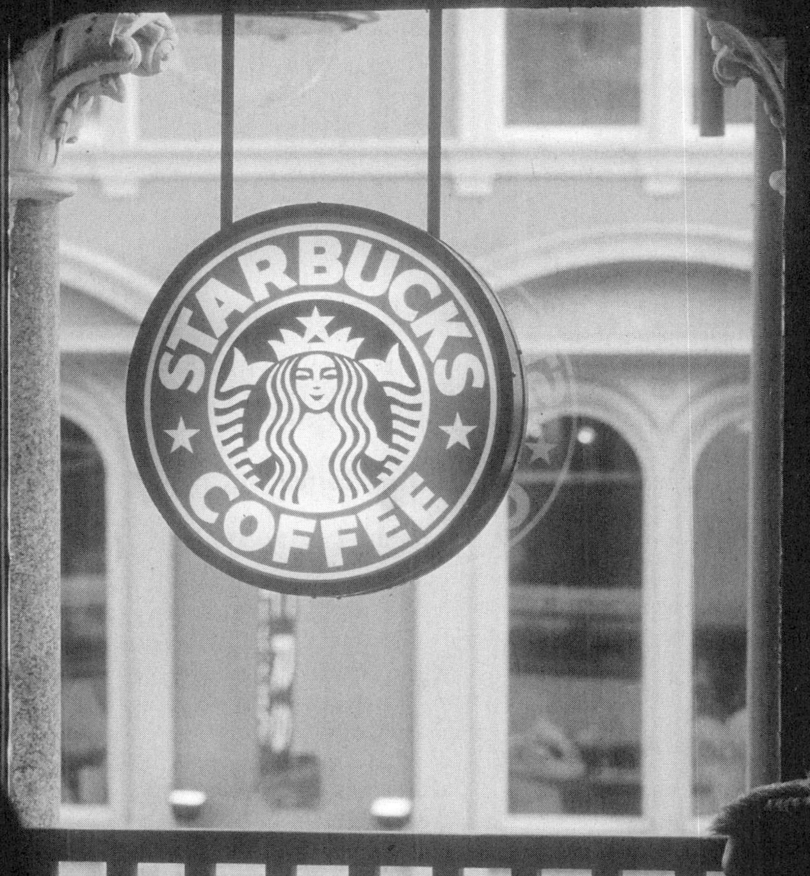

Europeans got their first Starbucks store in 1998.

the Starbucks name. Schultz dropped "teas and spices" from the logo, leaving it simply Starbucks Coffee (officially called Starbucks Corporation). He also had the logo changed from coffee-brown to green, white, and black and updated the two-tailed mermaid image.

Schultz wasted no time expanding his business. By the end of 1987, Starbucks had a total of 17 coffee bars, including more stores in Seattle, one in Vancouver, British Columbia—the first Starbucks outside the United States—and a few in

TAKEAWAY

Three years later, Starbucks had expanded its Seattle headquarters and had 84 stores up and running. By 1991, the company had moved into California, where its profits picked up considerably.

Chicago, Illinois. And that was just the beginning. Only three years later, Starbucks had expanded its Seattle headquarters and had 84 stores up and running. By 1991, the company had moved into California, where its profits picked up considerably.

Schultz had always aimed to create a company that respected and provided for its employees. So, in 1988, a year after buying Starbucks, he had begun offering full health benefits to eligible employees and their spouses. Next, in 1991, Starbucks set up a **stock options** program for full- and part-time employees. At the time, no other privately owned U.S. company had any such thing. Many more socially conscious acts were to come from Starbucks as it grew, including tuition assistance and paid time off for new parents.

June 26, 1992, marked another momentous occasion. Schultz called it the happiest day of his business career. Starbucks had lost money in the years after Schultz took over as chief **executive** officer (CEO). But profits from the many California stores had finally changed all that. Starbucks executives were now ready to turn their private company into a public one. On June 26, Starbucks was listed on the **stock market.** That meant anyone could buy shares in the company.

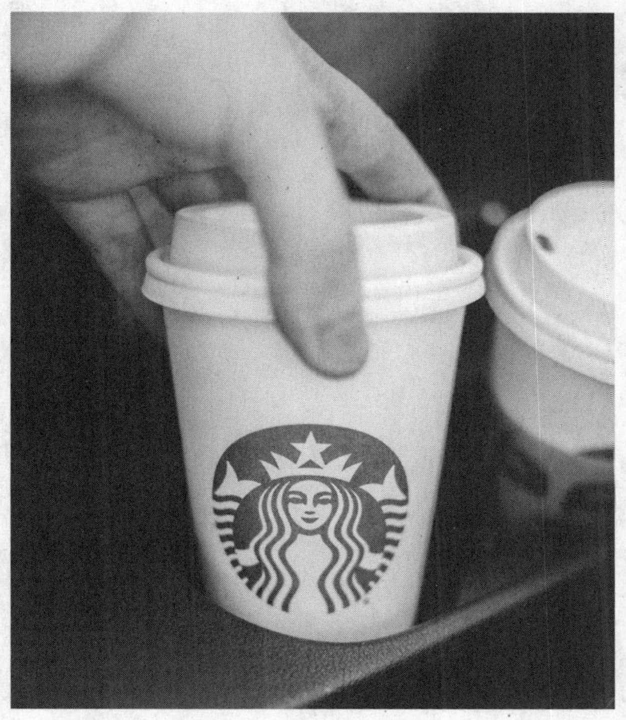

The decision paid off. Starbucks quickly raised $29 million in investor money and saw an increase in its value to $273 million. This was big news for a company that hadn't opened even a single espresso bar east of Chicago. East Coasters had barely even heard of Starbucks, let alone tasted its irresistible brew.

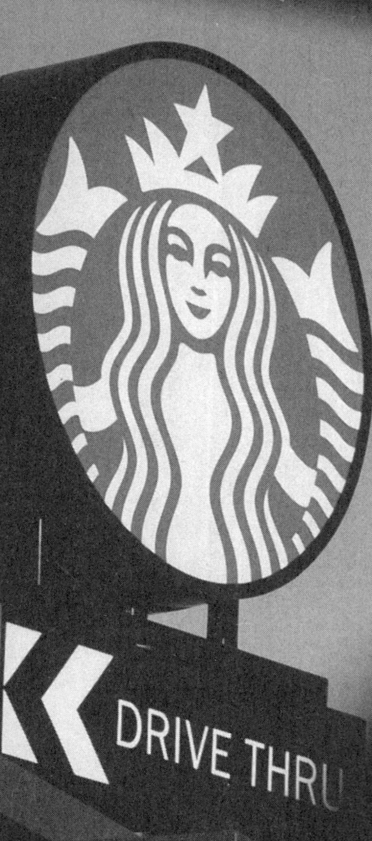
DRIVE THRU

Rapid Expansion

When Howard Schultz took over at Starbucks in 1987, he shared his big goal with employees: to make Starbucks a well-known, nationwide brand. To his investors, he was more specific: to have 125 Starbucks espresso bars up and running within five years.

OPPOSITE: Started as a walk-in-only store, Starbucks opened its first drive-through in 1994, in southern California.

But Schultz had already beaten that goal by 1992. Open stores numbered 167. Schultz had plenty of money to finance his further ambitions. It was time to expand to the East Coast.

Starbucks invaded Washington, D.C., first. It made sense to start there, for a couple reasons. The home office got consistently high numbers of coffee bean orders from the region. Also, many Europeans lived and worked in the city and surrounding areas. The choice proved to be a good one. The second D.C. Starbucks, which opened in the lively DuPont Circle neighborhood, especially stood out. In time, it did more business than most other stores across the entire country.

The early 1990s were a time of dynamic growth for Starbucks. Stores were opening all across the country now. People in Minneapolis, Minnesota; Houston and Dallas, Texas; Atlanta, Georgia; New York City; and Boston, Massachusetts, could all get a taste. Demand for fresh roasted beans was so high that two new roasting plants opened, one in Kent, Washington, and the other in York, Pennsylvania. Starbucks also opened its first drive-through store and an airport store at Seattle's Sea-Tac International. Sales were soaring! But then the company hit a snag. In 1994, a series of frosts destroyed acres of crops across Brazil's coffee plantations. This, in turn,

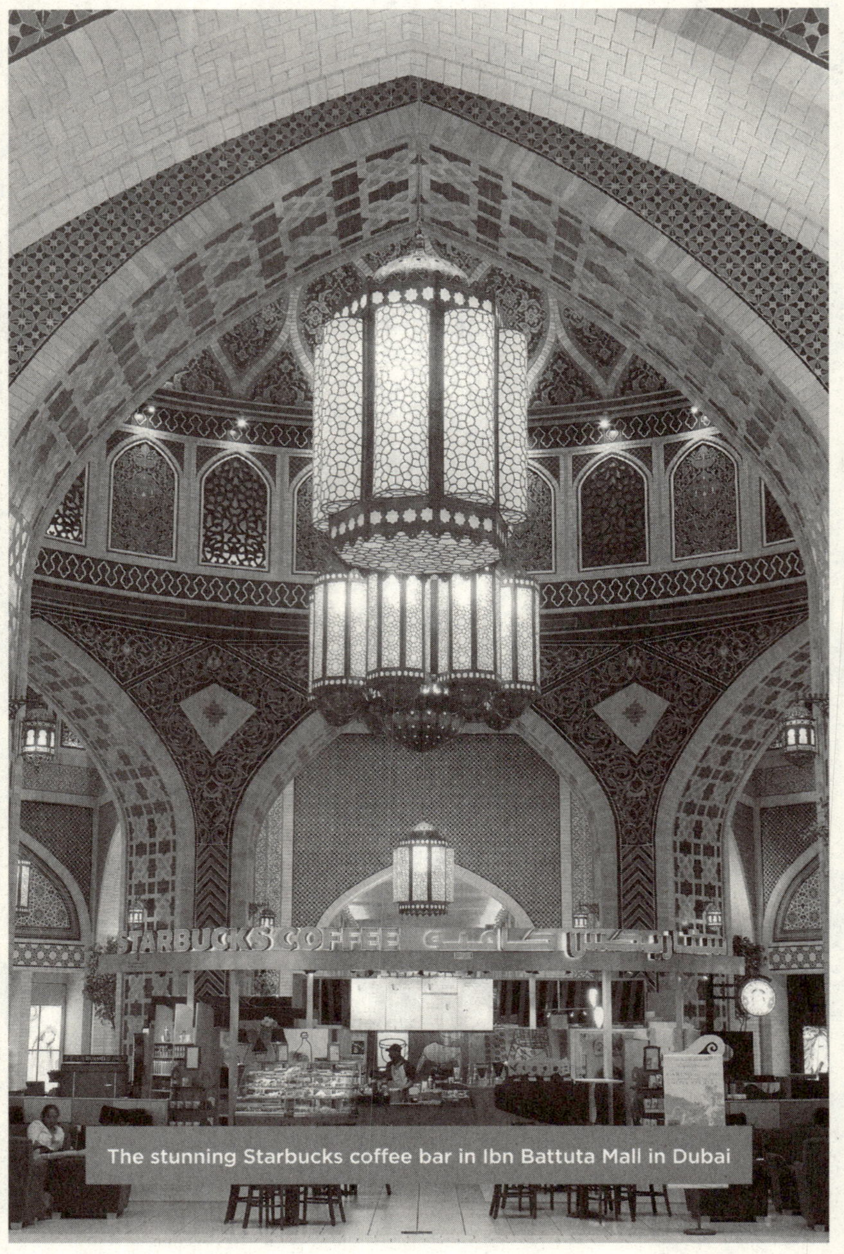

The stunning Starbucks coffee bar in Ibn Battuta Mall in Dubai

drove up bean prices, which affected Starbucks's prices and sales.

On the upside, the company already had a year's supply of beans bought at the lower prices. The downside was that investors were losing money because of the disaster, and the coming year would bring higher costs for operating.

Starbucks did raise its prices slightly—only 10 percent for most of its drinks. Beans increased in price by more than $1 per pound. But despite higher-costing coffee, Starbucks customers remained loyal to the brand because, Schultz believed, his coffee was "best of class." Customers weren't ready to jump ship for cheaper brew. Ultimately, even with the higher prices, Starbucks weathered the storm and kept on conquering.

By 1995, the company claimed a total of 677 coffee bars in North America, with about one store opening per day. That year was also notable for the introduction of a few new products. Starbucks super-premium ice cream was one. Music CDs were another. The third was a line of Frappuccino cold blended coffee drinks, which soon became wildly popular.

With things looking so solid, it was time to take Starbucks to the international stage. Japan was the

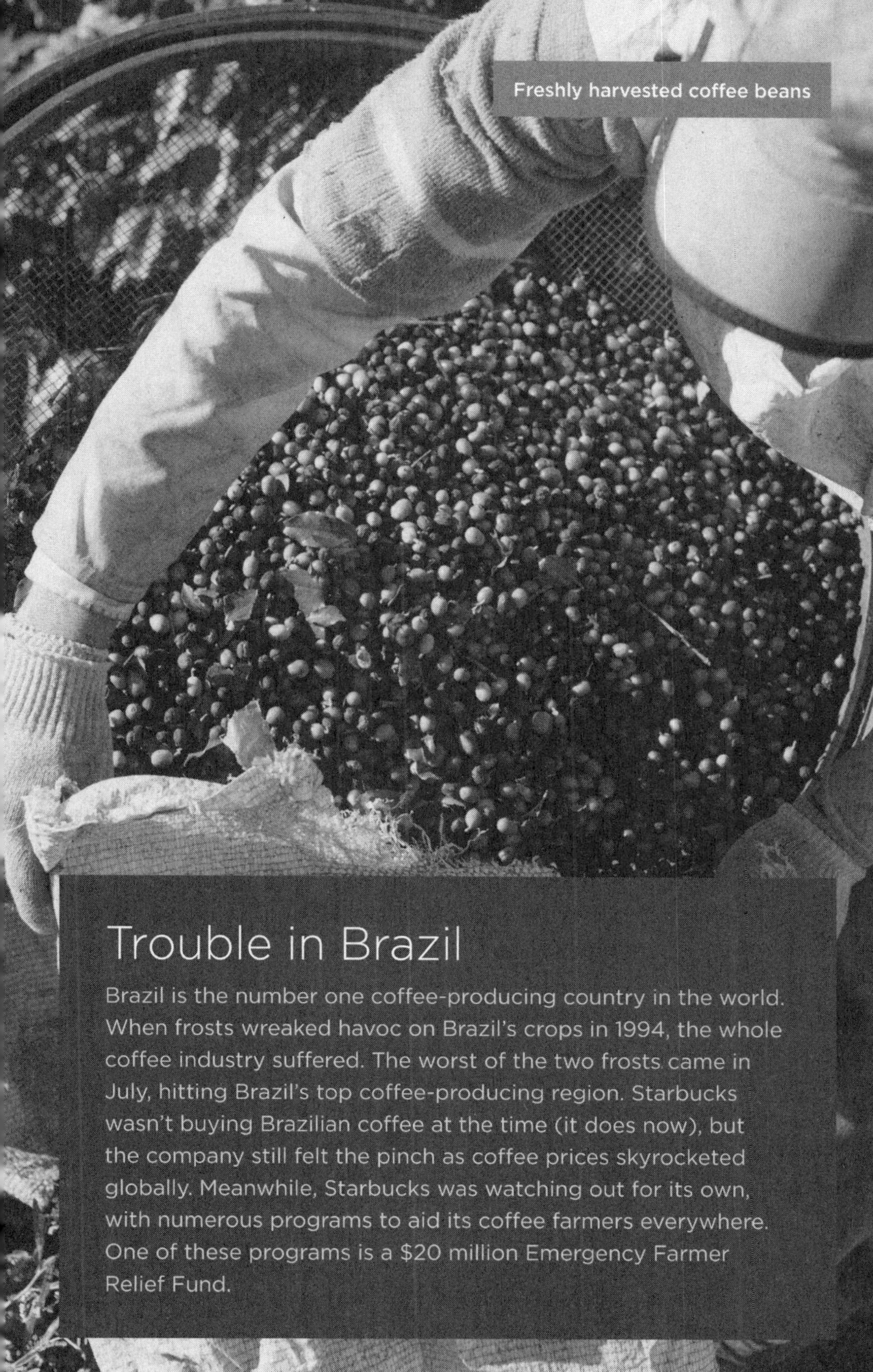

Freshly harvested coffee beans

Trouble in Brazil

Brazil is the number one coffee-producing country in the world. When frosts wreaked havoc on Brazil's crops in 1994, the whole coffee industry suffered. The worst of the two frosts came in July, hitting Brazil's top coffee-producing region. Starbucks wasn't buying Brazilian coffee at the time (it does now), but the company still felt the pinch as coffee prices skyrocketed globally. Meanwhile, Starbucks was watching out for its own, with numerous programs to aid its coffee farmers everywhere. One of these programs is a $20 million Emergency Farmer Relief Fund.

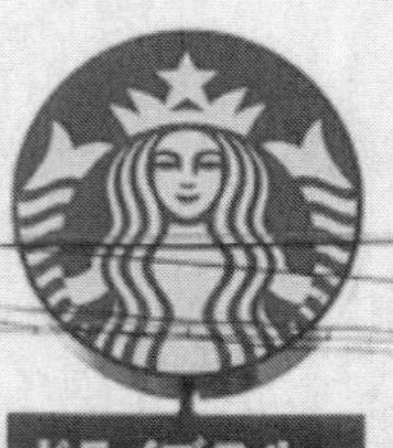

As of 2023, Japan had more than 1,550 Starbucks stores.

company's first target. Moving into an Eastern culture presented new opportunities, challenges, and questions. *In addition to coffee, would Starbucks offer tea to honor the country's traditional tea culture? Would anyone buy coffee?*

Tea *was* on the menu at the first Japanese Starbucks store, which opened on August 2, 1996, in Tokyo. Schultz was there that sweltering summer day. He witnessed dozens of people lining up to buy tea, lattes, and hot espresso drinks. Coffee was still the store's main attraction. After all, at that time,

Japan was the world's fifth largest coffee importer. But Starbucks had joined forces with Sazaby, Inc., a company well known throughout Japan for its high-end retail outlets and restaurant chains. Sazaby's role was to guide Starbucks as it moved into an entirely new cultural landscape. Thus, tea was still an essential.

The **joint venture** looked good from the start. Starbucks executives had projected Starbucks Coffee Japan to become profitable by 2002. In fact, that goal was achieved by 2000. Proudly claiming it had started a trend, Starbucks gener-

TAKEAWAY

By 1995, the company claimed a total of 677 coffee bars in North America, with about one store opening per day.

ated considerable interest throughout Japan. This wasn't all a good thing, though. In 2002, the company suffered a loss of $3.9 million in Japan, its second largest market. The dive was caused mainly by the speedy growth of competing and copying coffee businesses.

Nevertheless, Starbucks continued to expand. In 1997, it appeared in the Philippines. The next year, it opened in the United Kingdom, New Zealand, Thailand, Taiwan, and Malaysia. In 1999, it landed in Lebanon, Kuwait, China, and South Korea. By the turn of the century, Starbucks had 2,498 stores around the globe.

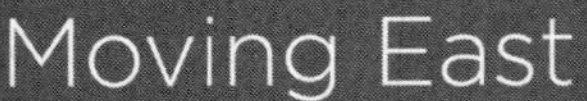

Moving East

Wisely, Starbucks did its homework before expanding into Japan. It found that Japanese customers preferred drinks in smaller portions and with much less sugar than Americans liked. Drink recipes and serving sizes were changed accordingly. Because tea drinking is as much a way of life in Japanese culture as espresso drinking in Italy, matcha and other tea drinks were added to the menu. Also, in Japan's very polite culture, shouting out a customer's name would have been rude, so baristas assigned every order a number instead to let customers know when their drinks were ready.

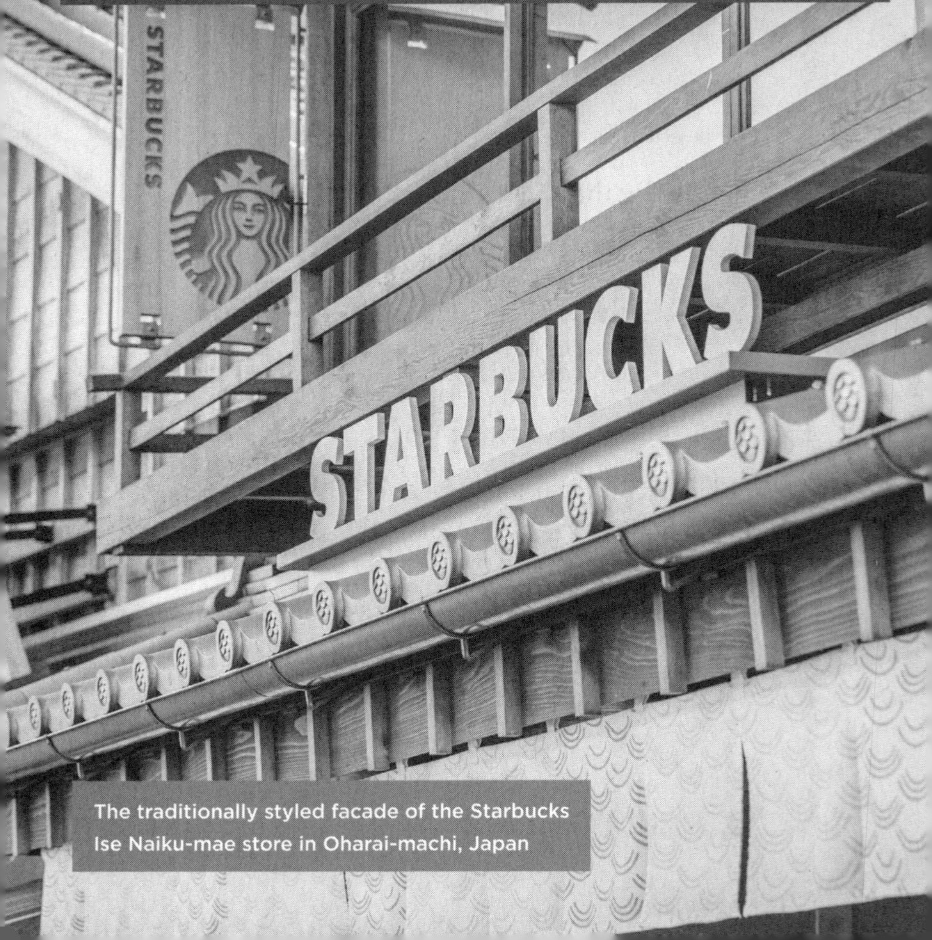

The traditionally styled facade of the Starbucks Ise Naiku-mae store in Oharai-machi, Japan

Coffee bars weren't Starbucks's only venture, though. In 1998, Starbucks products had been introduced into grocery stores. The Starbucks.com website was launched the same year. The company also bought Tazo tea company in 1998.

Schultz found ways for Starbucks to contribute to people and the planet as well. The Starbucks Foundation was established in 1997 to support various literacy programs in the United States. To promote **sustainable** coffee-growing practices, Starbucks partnered with the environmental nonprofit Conservation International in 1999. In 2000, the

OPPOSITE Some Starbucks stores in Japan blend seamlessly with local architectural styles.

company made an agreement to sell Fairtrade-certified coffee in the United States and Canada. This kind of agreement makes sure coffee farmers are paid a living wage and ensures other benefits for workers in the coffee industry.

The year 2000 brought big changes for Schultz personally, as well. After 13 years as CEO, he stepped down to become Starbucks's chairman and chief global **strategist**. As such, his focus was on expanding international business, particularly in China. In 2000 alone, Starbucks began doing business in Hong Kong, Australia, the United Arab Emirates, Bahrain, and Saudi Arabia.

The next few years brought more new developments. Starbucks established new roasting plants around the world. It offered free Wi-Fi and partnered with Apple in 2007. Because of this

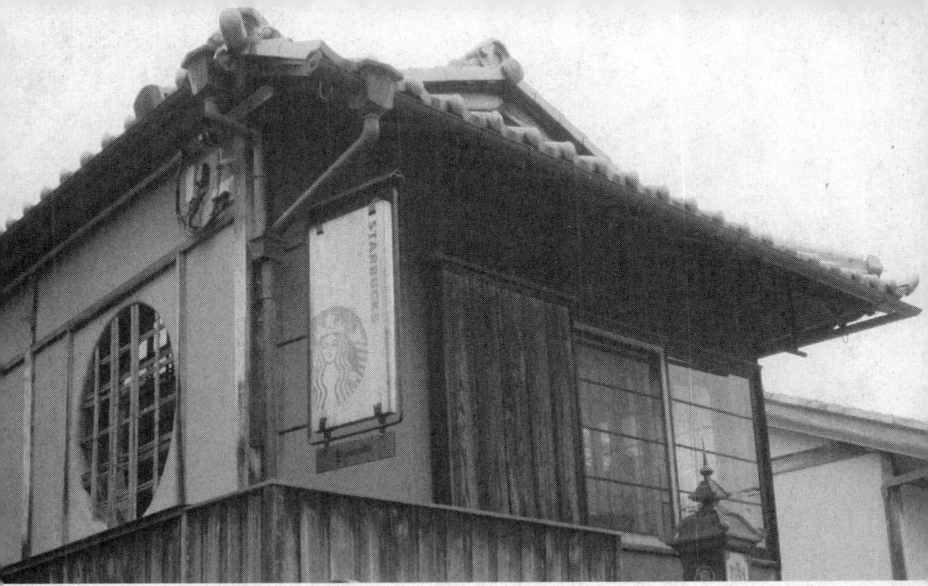

partnership, when customers entered Starbucks, their devices would automatically connect to the iTunes Wi-Fi Music Store. As well as listening to and buying tunes, users could identify the music playing right then inside the store.

Seeking further ways to be more environmentally friendly, the company started including recycled materials in its cups. It also introduced water-saving practices into its coffee-making process. It was a new millennium, and Starbucks seemed to be riding high. But more business shake-ups were brewing.

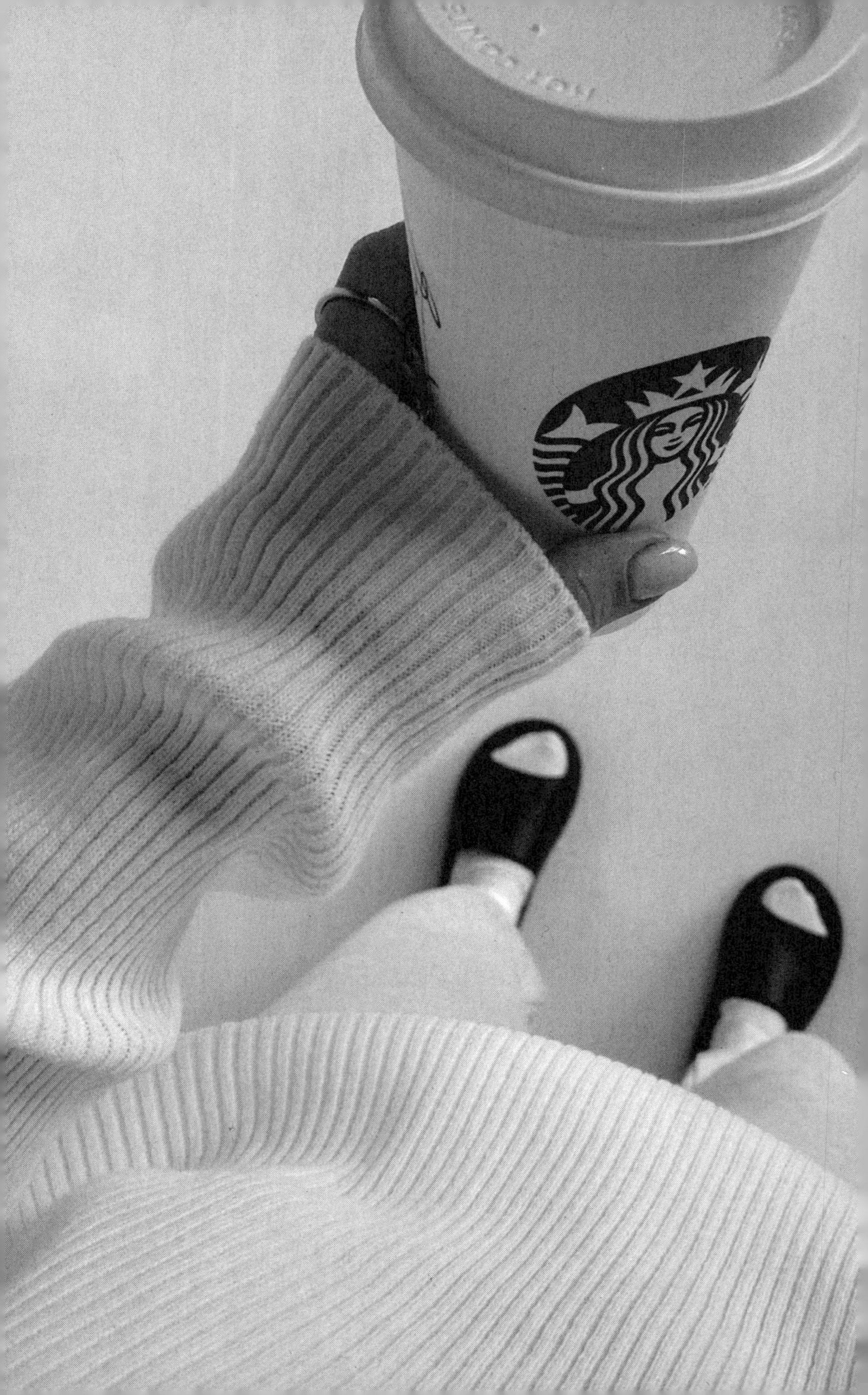

Commitment and Controversy

As the first decade of the 2000s approached its end, the world began to wobble. In December 2007, a severe **recession** hit the United States and soon spread around the globe. Businesses were in financial crisis for the next two years. Starbucks suffered, too. The company closed 900 stores and laid off around 6,700 employees.

OPPOSITE: During the economic downturn of the late 2000s, customers tightened their wallets and bought fewer "expensive" coffees such as Starbucks.

In Howard Schultz's opinion, though, the recession hadn't caused Starbucks's problems. Neither had the coffee prices. Schultz believed the company's woes had more to do with losing its "soul"—its focus on giving customers the best possible experience. Starbucks had increased efficiency, for instance, by creating procedures for making drinks much quicker. But the personal barista-customer connection seemed to have gone missing.

In 2008, Schultz swooped in like a superhero to save the day. Returning as CEO, he swiftly made changes. He hired, fired, and assigned

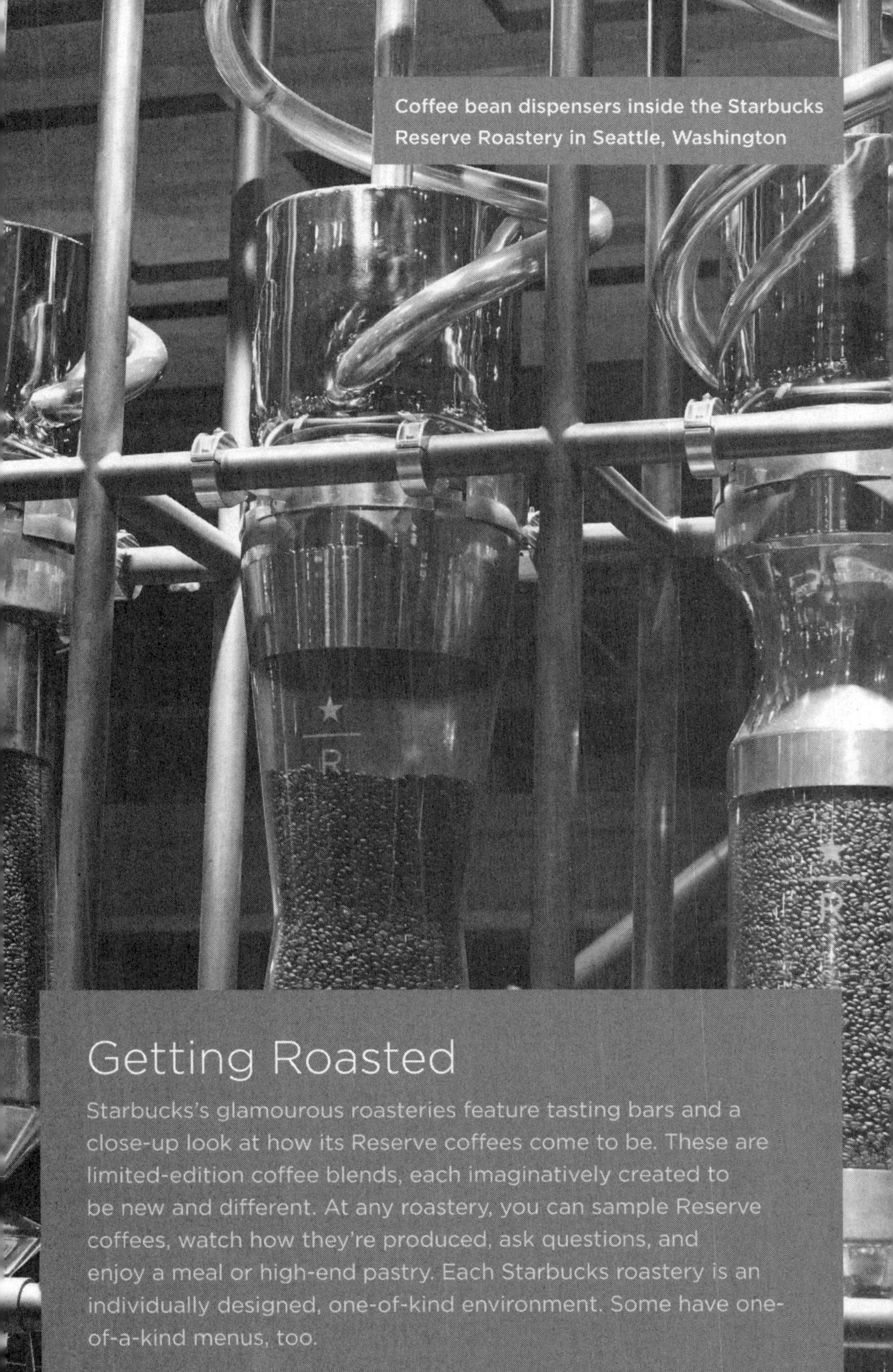

Coffee bean dispensers inside the Starbucks Reserve Roastery in Seattle, Washington

Getting Roasted

Starbucks's glamourous roasteries feature tasting bars and a close-up look at how its Reserve coffees come to be. These are limited-edition coffee blends, each imaginatively created to be new and different. At any roastery, you can sample Reserve coffees, watch how they're produced, ask questions, and enjoy a meal or high-end pastry. Each Starbucks roastery is an individually designed, one-of-kind environment. Some have one-of-a-kind menus, too.

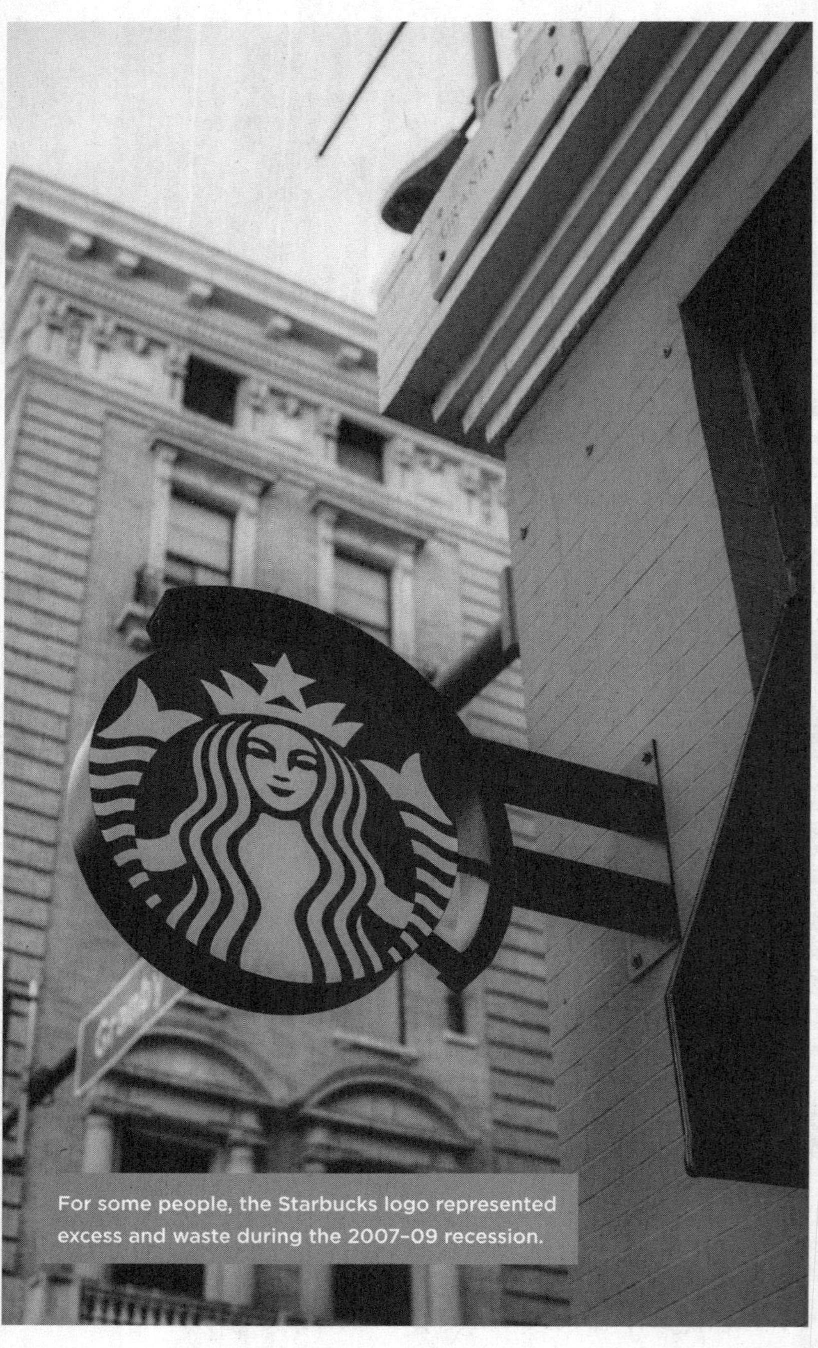

For some people, the Starbucks logo represented excess and waste during the 2007–09 recession.

new roles. Schultz's plan to revitalize Starbucks had three parts: strengthen the company by focusing on its core mission, customer satisfaction; find ways to improve the in-store customer experience; and take action to grow the business even further.

One early aspect of this plan was the My Starbucks Idea program, launched in 2008. On the program's website, Starbucks fans could give direct input to the company's decision-makers. People freely offered ideas, suggestions, complaints, and praise. Starbucks listened and responded, making the site a strong community

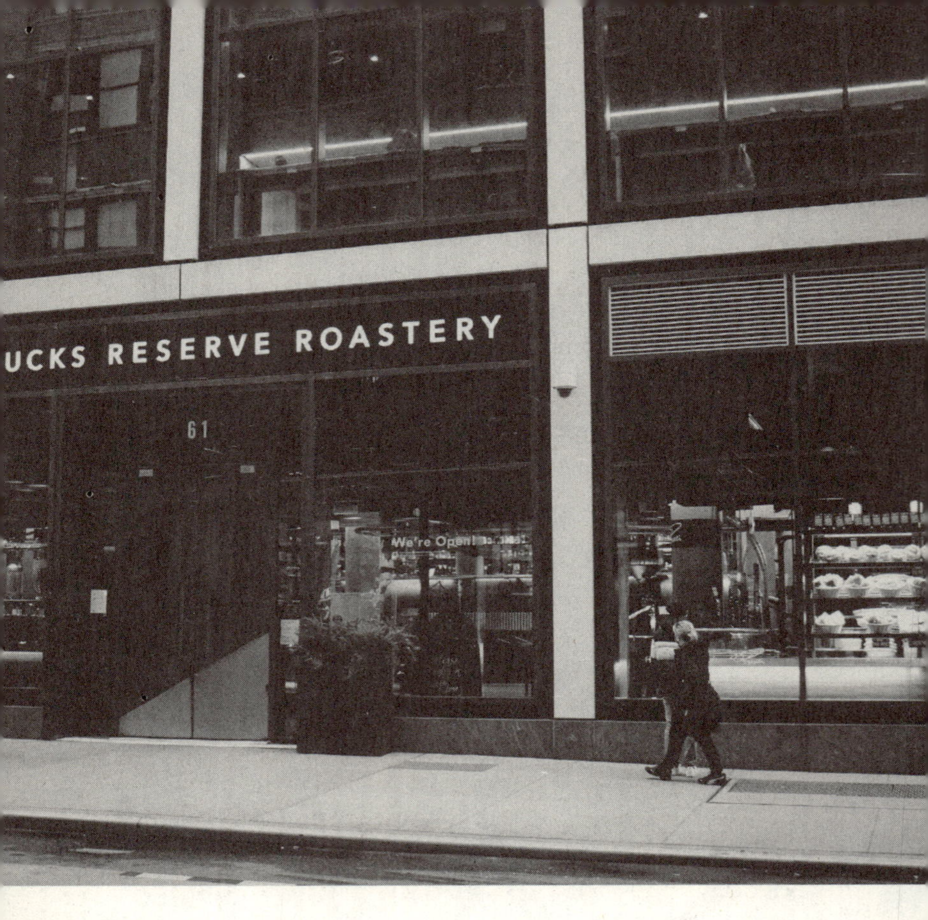

builder. According to Starbucks, 275 customer ideas were put into action between 2008 and 2013. Some of these ideas involved new services, new products, and changes due to complaints. Ultimately, this public forum created even greater

OPPOSITE Howard Schultz had the idea for Starbucks Reserve Roasteries, which elevated coffee making to an art form.

brand loyalty. And Starbucks's own loyalty to its customers, shown by listening and taking action, paid off as well.

Under Schultz's leadership, the focused efforts to improve things at Starbucks were generally a tremendous success. In 2016 alone, financial reports showed company profits up 22 percent. By then, Starbucks was doing business in 75 countries outside of North America, with a total of 25,085 stores and about 300,000 employees. Between 2011 and 2017, the company opened

10,000 new stores, thousands of them in China. Business was booming again.

Starbucks was also going in new and interesting directions. In 2014, Schultz fulfilled a decades-long dream for the company. That year in Seattle, the first-ever Starbucks Reserve Roastery opened a few blocks from the original Starbucks site. There, customers could catch a behind-the-scenes glimpse of the company's step-by-step coffee operation. The Roastery showcased exactly how Starbucks sources, roasts, and crafts its coffee.

The concept caught on and spread. In 2017, Schultz once again gave up his CEO position, this time to focus on opening more Roasteries. The second one landed in Shanghai, China, in 2017. Then, in September 2018, Starbucks hit a major milestone. A big, beautiful, and very posh Starbucks

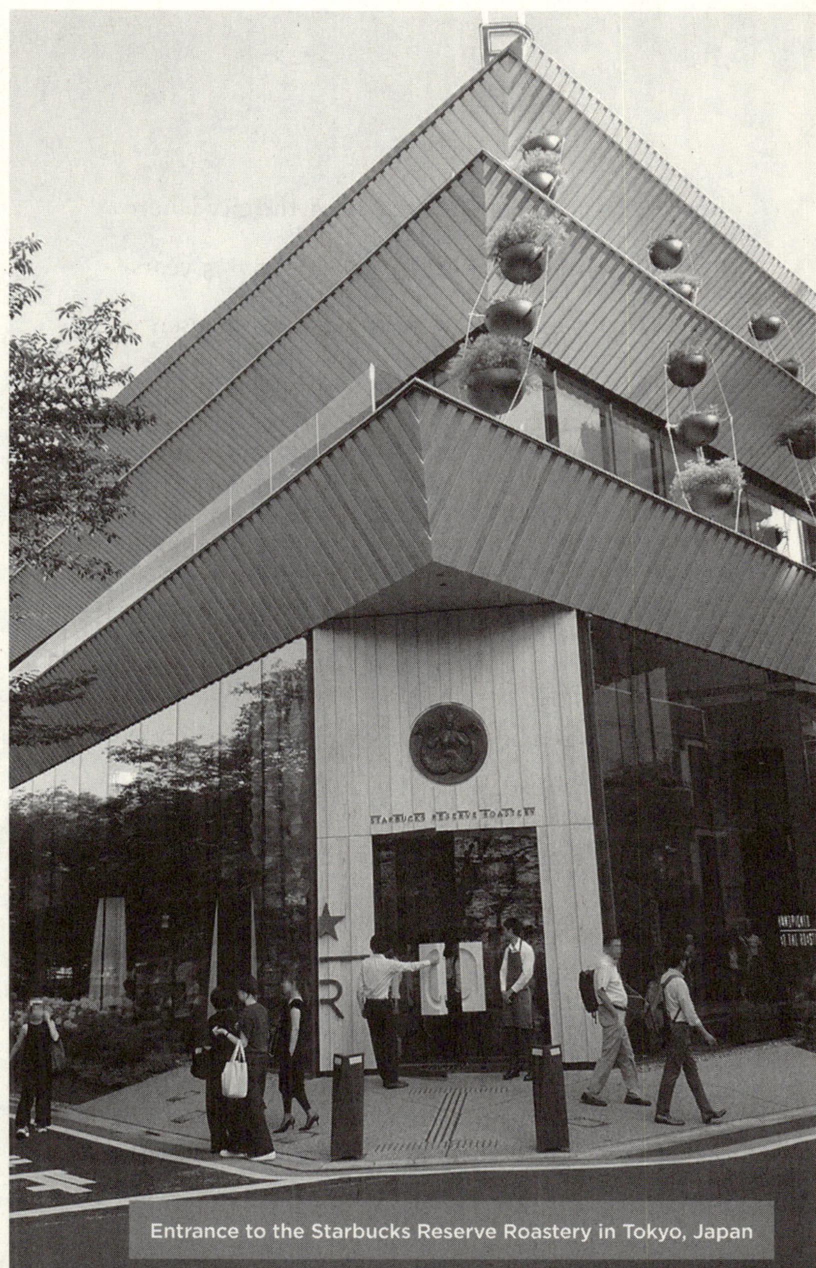

Entrance to the Starbucks Reserve Roastery in Tokyo, Japan

Reserve Roastery opened in Milan, the city where it had all started for Schultz. After nearly 35 years, he had finally managed to give Starbucks a presence in Italy. Today, there are six Starbucks Reserve Roasteries globally. The others opened in New York City (2018), Tokyo (2019), and on Chicago's Miracle Mile (2019)—a five-story building that is the largest Starbucks in the world.

In 2020, during the COVID-19 pandemic, Starbucks took a big hit, along with countless other businesses. The lockdown forced the closure of many stores that didn't have a drive-through feature. Pickups and delivery orders became common, and sales fell. Stores that stayed open followed strict safety measures. Starbucks spent $10 million to set up the Starbucks Global Partner Emergency Relief program. It supported U.S. and Canadian food banks throughout the pandemic. The Starbucks Foundation donated more than $3 million to support worldwide COVID-19 relief efforts. The company contributed generously to public well-being in countless other ways, too.

As the global health crisis slowly resolved, and things began opening again, people flocked to Starbucks stores. Customers sought community and connection. But drive-through, pickup, and delivery orders remained as important services. This new, more flexible way of serving customers was a big plus. Starbucks experienced record-breaking financial gains as restrictions began to lift.

These changes reflect Starbucks's drive to continually expand, renew, and improve. Other **initiatives** have included creating partnership deals with Pepsi and other companies. Starbucks has bought other businesses to expand its offerings. Over many years, it has been especially focused on adopting more socially aware practices, including ongoing aid to its coffee farmers.

Starbucks is not without **controversy**, however. Under Schultz's leadership, its stores are meant to

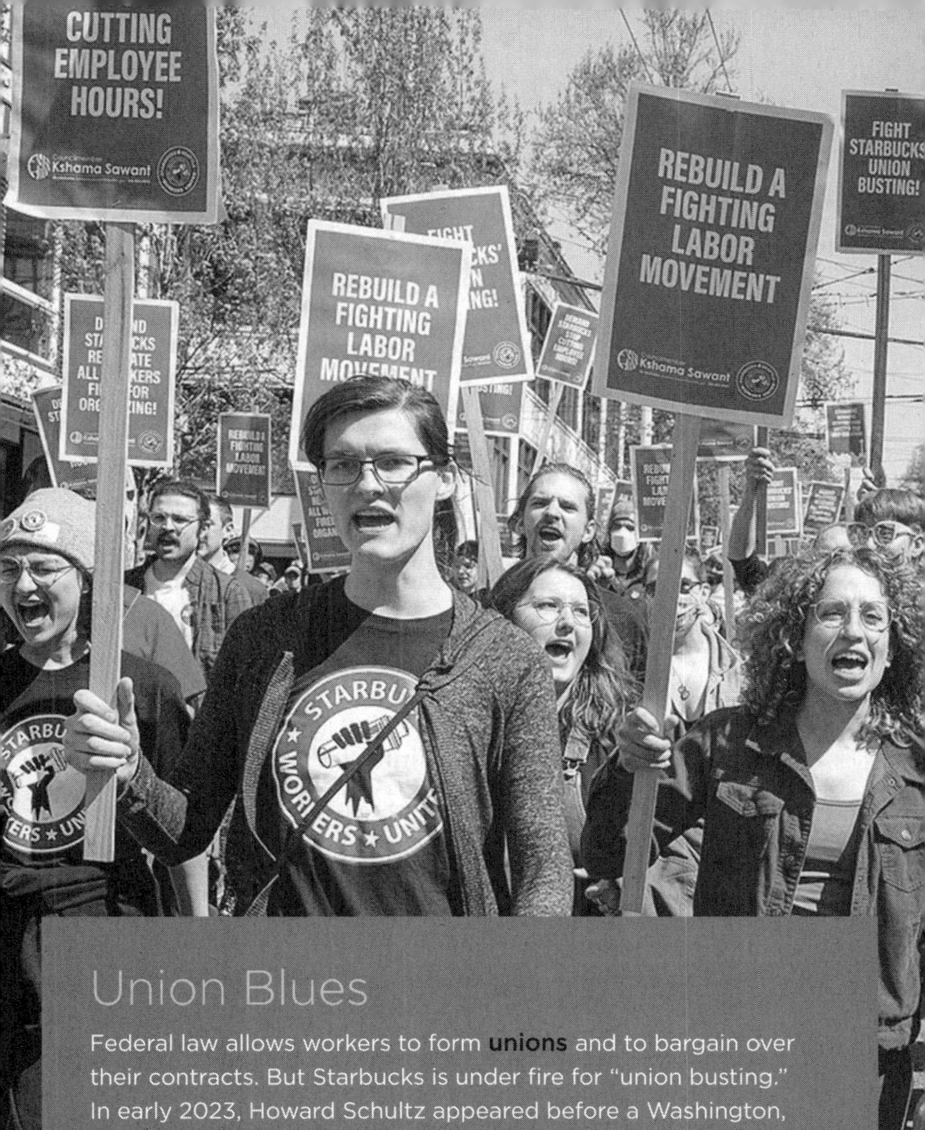

Union Blues

Federal law allows workers to form **unions** and to bargain over their contracts. But Starbucks is under fire for "union busting." In early 2023, Howard Schultz appeared before a Washington, D.C., Senate committee to answer questions about these claims. To almost every question, Schultz replied, "I support the law, and I also take offense with you categorizing me or Starbucks as a union buster when that is not true." But a judge in Buffalo, New York, had earlier ruled that Starbucks *had* broken labor laws, many times. Nevertheless, Schultz said he would not carry out the Labor Board's demands because he "hadn't broken the law."

be places with a strong sense of community. The company strives to be a do-good, socially responsive leader. But Starbucks has sparked public outrage more than once. One of the most intense outcries has been over apparent **racial profiling** on the part of some employees and the consequences of these actions. After one highly publicized store incident, the company closed more than 8,000 U.S. stores for four hours to hold anti-**bias** training for employees.

Another ongoing issue for Starbucks is what many people consider the company's anti-union position. Since 2021, Starbucks employees have worked to unionize in more than 250 stores across 40 states. But their efforts have met resistance from management. Around the time of Schultz's 2008 return as CEO, he said he wanted to "make sure people realize the deep level of respect we have for the work [the employees] do." He has also said, "I would listen to [employees'] concerns. If they had faith in me and my motives, they wouldn't need a union." But today, Schultz's attitude seems clearly anti-union. And Starbucks Workers United seems to be gathering strength.

In recent years, some Starbucks employees have been fired for trying to organize unions. The company has received formal complaints from the National Labor Relations Board. In part, the complaints state that Starbucks took actions against individuals who supported unionization. Only time will tell if Starbucks's anti-union stance will damage its good reputation.

The coffee giant has weathered many storms since Schultz first took charge in 1987. It has shown its commitment to the communities it serves by contributing in positive ways all around the world. It has put millions of dollars into important social causes. And, of course, it has spent decades offering its superior coffee-based experience to customers everywhere.

Howard Schultz assumed the position of interim CEO for Starbucks in 2022 and stepped down for the third and final time in early 2023. But the biggest, most successful coffee brand ever will always be associated with Schultz and his global vision. What comes next for the company is anyone's guess. Whatever happens, it seems certain that the Starbucks brand won't lose its leader-of-the-pack status anytime soon.

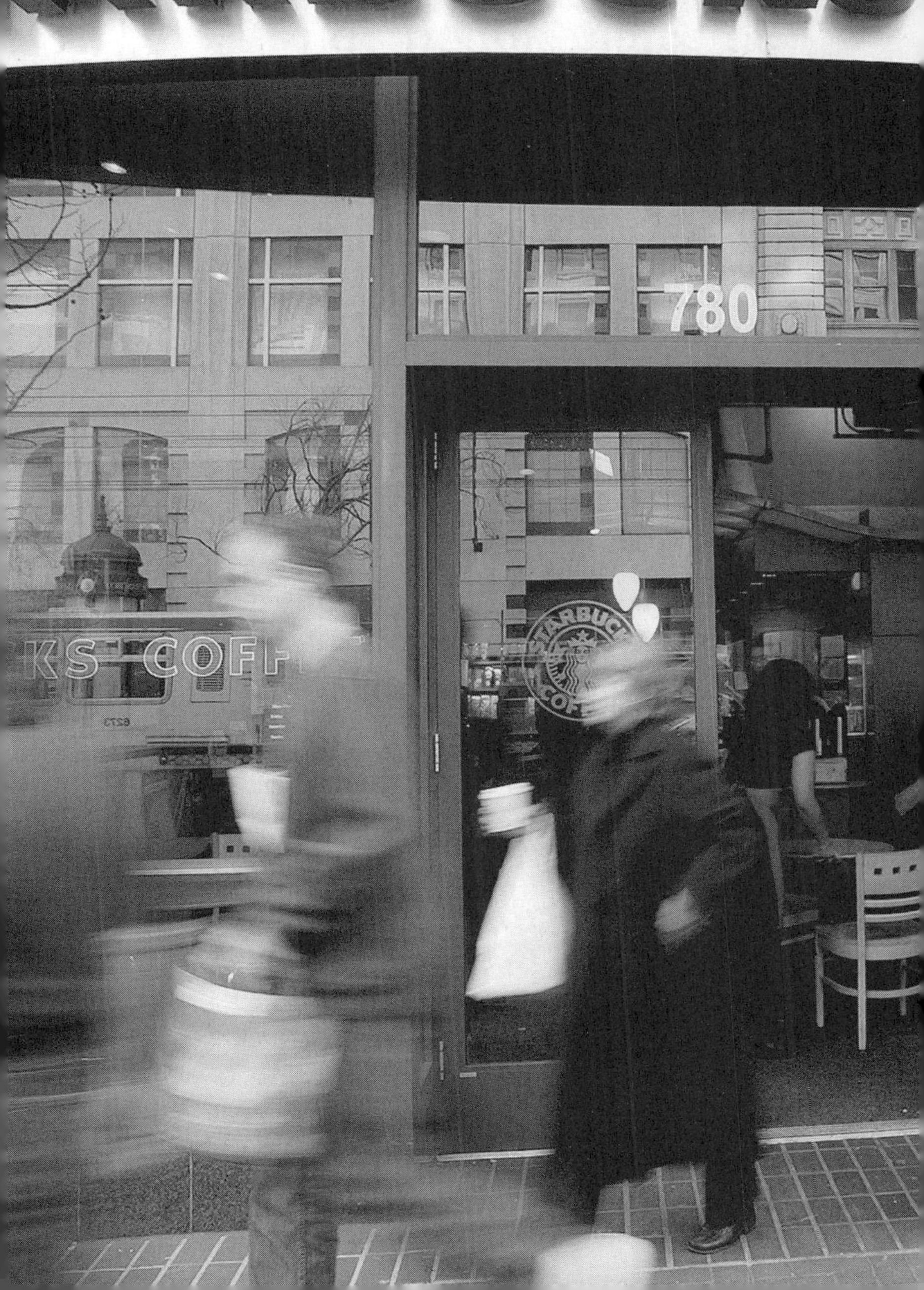
ARBUCKS
780

Selected Bibliography

Behar, Howard, with Janet Goldstein. *It's Not About the Coffee: Leadership Principles from a Life at Starbucks.* New York: Portfolio, 2007.

Farr, Sheila. "Starbucks: The Early Years." HistoryLink.org. February 15, 2017. https://www.historylink.org/file/20292.

Haddon, Heather. "Starbucks Is Rethinking Almost Everything, Including How to Make Frappuccinos." *Wall Street Journal.* August 31, 2022. https://www.wsj.com/articles/starbucks-howard-schultz-change-frappuccinos-11661888871.

---. "Starbucks's Howard Schultz: From Coffee Entrepreneur to Three-Time CEO." *Wall Street Journal.* April 1, 2022. https://www.wsj.com/story/starbuckss-howard-schultz-from-coffee-entrepreneur-to-three-time-ceo-439768fc.

Rainey, Clint. "What Happened to Starbucks? How a Progressive Company Lost Its Way." *Fast Company.* March 17, 2022. https://www.fastcompany.com/90732166/what-happened-to-starbucks-how-a-progressive-company-lost-its-way.

Schultz, Howard, and Dori Jones Yang. *Pour Your Heart into It: How Starbucks Built a Company One Cup at a Time.* New York: Hyperion, 1997.

Schultz, Howard, with Joanne Gordon. *Onward: How Starbucks Fought for Its Life Without Losing Its Soul.* New York: Rodale, 2011.

Glossary

barista — an Italian word for someone who makes and serves coffee and espresso-based drinks to customers

bias — a prejudice against or in favor of a group, person, or thing, often unfairly

controversy — a disagreement that is usually public and taking place over time

espresso — a strong, concentrated coffee brewed by forcing steam through darkly roasted ground coffee beans

executive — a decision-making leader of a company, such as a president or chief executive officer (CEO)

investor — a person or company that commits money or other resources in order to earn a financial return

joint venture — a contractual agreement joining together two or more parties to complete a business undertaking; all parties share in whatever profits or losses result

profit — the amount of money that a business keeps after subtracting expenses from revenues

racial profiling — using a person's race or ethnicity as a reason to suspect them of having committed an offense

recession a period of decline in the economy, resulting in less trade and business and increasing financial hardship for some

seed money funds used to start a new business or project

stock market the public place where people buy and sell company shares, or portions of shared ownership (stock)

stock option an opportunity for employees or investors in a company to buy or sell that company's stock; stock options are often given as part of an employee's benefits package

strategist someone who figures out the best plan to help a business or organization reach its goals

sustainable able to continue over a long period of time; ways of operating that help keep the environment safe and healthy

union an organized group of workers formed to protect their interests and rights as employees

wholesale related to buying or selling goods in large quantities at low prices, which are then usually sold in retail stores or other settings at a higher price

Websites

Becoming Resource Positive
https://www.starbucks.com/responsibility/planet
Learn how Starbucks is trying to give more than it takes from the planet.

Starbucks Archive
https://archive.starbucks.com
Explore company milestones through a collection of timelines and people profiles.

Starbucks Stories & News
https://stories.starbucks.com
Read a wide range of articles about every part of Starbucks, from its people and coffee craft to its newest products.

Index

More Titles from the Creative Companies Series

Jaico's creative companies series explores how today's great companies operate and inspires young readers to become the entrepreneurs and businessmen of tomorrow.

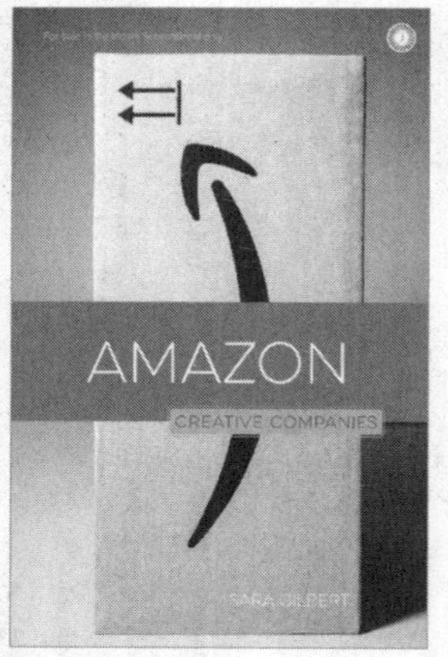

Amazon

Jeff Bezos founded Amazon in 1994 in a garage in Seattle, Washington, as an online bookstore. On July 16, 1995, Bezos launched the site, named after the vast Amazon River, and invited 300 friends to beta test it. Within 30 days, Amazon sold books across the U.S. and 45 countries, achieving meteoric success without press promotion. Today, Amazon is an e-commerce giant, offering a vast array of products and services while continuously innovating under Bezos's visionary leadership.

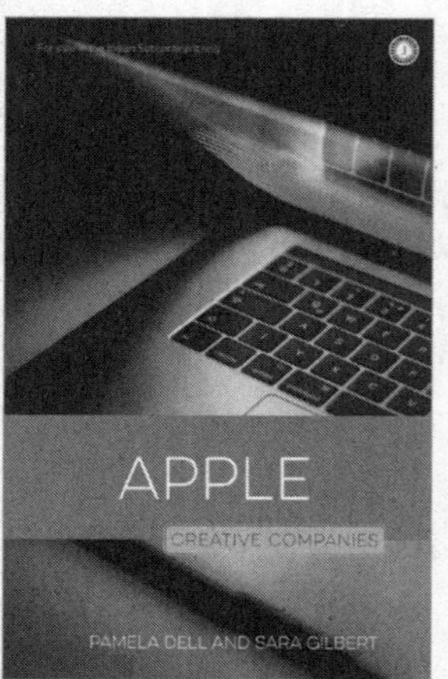

Apple

Did you know, Apple—the company behind your iPod, iPad, iPhone—began as a project shared by two ambitious boys in their computer club? When Steve Wozniak designed a computer in 1976, his friend Steve Jobs immediately saw its potential for a mass market. They found their first 'customer' at their local hobby club meeting and Apple Computer was born. Over the next 30-plus years, their company would transform the computer industry.

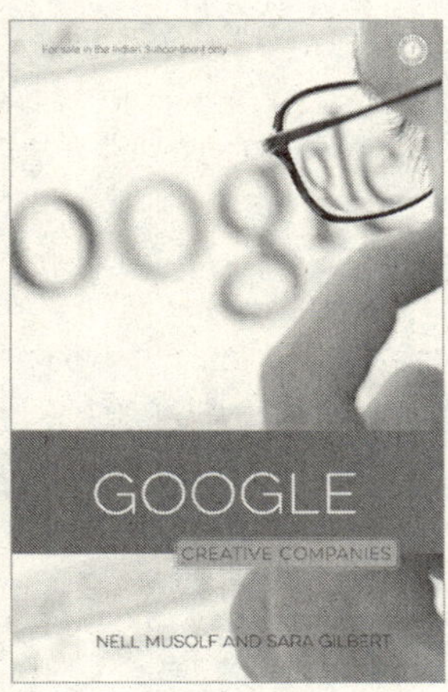

Google

This is the inspiring story of Larry Page and Sergey Brin, the founders of Google, who first met at Stanford University, in 1995. Most people would not even be aware of the fact that the very first Google office was in a friend's rented garage. Page and Brin soon began working on a likely doctoral thesis, which involved an attempt to download the complete World Wide Web, after which they would create a way to search the web, with the help of links. After many issues that involved budgeting and design, Google came into being.

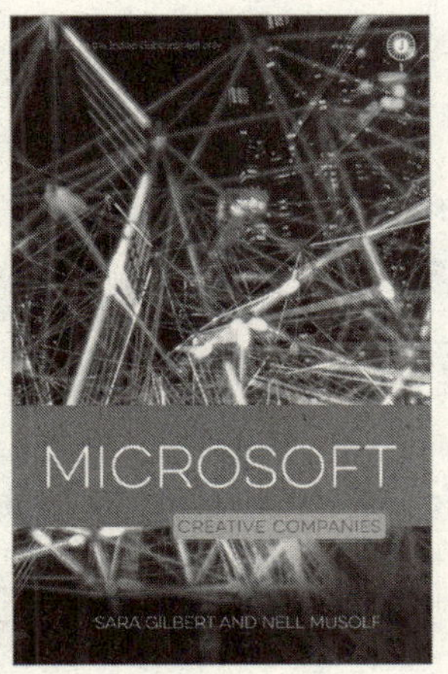

Microsoft

Bill Gates was in his second year of college at Harvard when he and his partner Paul Allen launched their own computer software company. Throughout their years at Lakeside School, Bill Gates and Paul Allen spent as much time as they could working on computers, becoming good friends in the process. Their company's impact has been such that the name 'Microsoft' has become virtually synonymous with computer software.

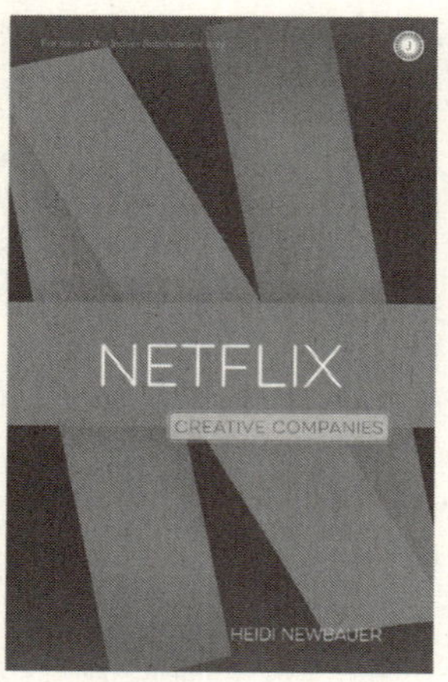

Netflix

Netflix was founded in 1997 by Reed Hastings and Marc Randolph in California as a DVD rental-by-mail service. Hastings was inspired after incurring a $40 late fee on a VHS rental, sparking the idea for a subscription-based model. In 2007, Netflix pivoted to online streaming, offering on-demand entertainment. By 2013, it expanded into original programming with hits like House of Cards. Today, Netflix is a global streaming powerhouse, revolutionizing how audiences consume movies and TV shows across the world.

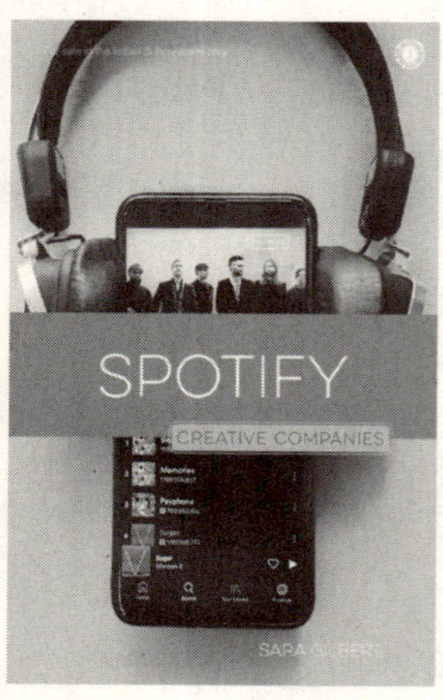

Spotify

Spotify was founded in 2006 by Daniel Ek and Martin Lorentzon in Stockholm, Sweden, as a response to music piracy. They envisioned a legal platform offering instant, affordable access to a vast music library. Launched in 2008, Spotify introduced a freemium model with ads and premium subscriptions. Its curated playlists and personalized recommendations reshaped music consumption. Today, Spotify is a global leader in audio streaming, boasting millions of tracks and podcasts, transforming how listeners discover and enjoy music worldwide..

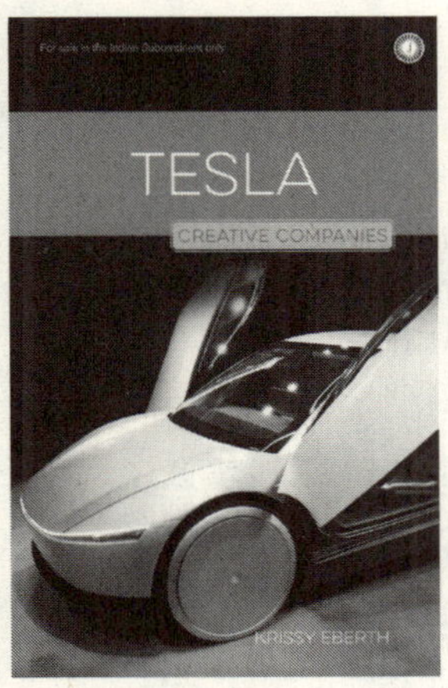

Tesla

Tesla was founded in 2003 by Martin Eberhard and Marc Tarpenning, with Elon Musk joining shortly after as an investor and chairman. Named after inventor Nikola Tesla, the company aimed to revolutionize transportation with electric vehicles. In 2008, Tesla launched the Roadster, proving EVs could be high-performance. Musk's leadership expanded Tesla's vision to sustainable energy solutions, including solar products and battery storage. Today, Tesla leads the EV industry, pushing innovation and advancements in autonomous driving.

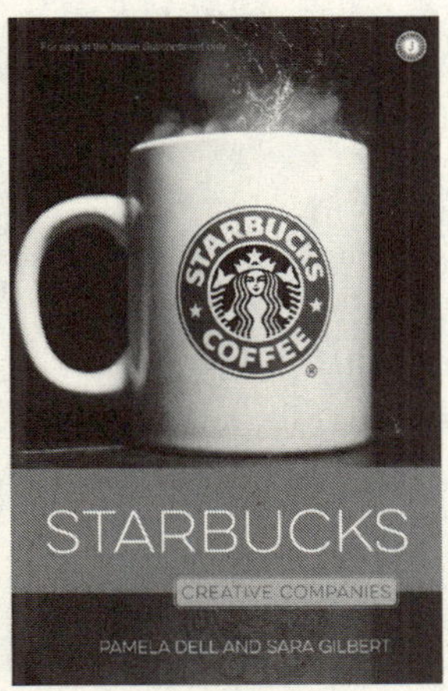

Starbucks

Starbucks was founded in 1971 by Jerry Baldwin, Zev Siegl, and Gordon Bowker in Seattle, Washington, as a single store selling high-quality coffee beans and equipment. Inspired by Italian coffee culture, Howard Schultz joined in 1982 and later transformed Starbucks into a café-centric brand, emphasizing premium coffee experiences. The first café opened in 1984, revolutionizing coffee consumption. Today, Starbucks operates thousands of locations globally.

JAICO PUBLISHING HOUSE
Elevate Your Life. Transform Your World.

ESTABLISHED IN 1946, Jaico Publishing House is home to world-transforming authors such as Robin Sharma, Sadhguru, Osho, the Dalai Lama, Deepak Chopra, Eknath Easwaran, Paramhansa Yogananda, Devdutt Pattanaik, Radhakrishnan Pillai, Morgan Housel, Napoleon Hill, John Maxwell, Brian Tracy, and Stephen Hawking.

Our late founder Mr. Jaman Shah first established Jaico as a book distribution company. Sensing that independence was around the corner, he aptly named his company Jaico ('Jai' means victory in Hindi). In order to service the significant demand for affordable books in a developing nation, Mr. Shah initiated Jaico's own publications. Jaico was India's first publisher of paperback books in the English language.

While self-help; religion and philosophy; mind, body and spirit; and business titles form the cornerstone of our non-fiction list, we publish an exciting range of current affairs, history, biography, art and architecture, travel, and popular science books as well. Our renewed focus on popular fiction is evident in our new titles by a host of fresh young talent from India and abroad.

Jaico's translations division publishes select bestselling titles in over 10 regional languages including Gujarati, Hindi, Kannada, Malayalam, Marathi, Tamil, and Telugu. These include titles from renowned national and international authors like Sudha Murthy, Gaur Gopal Das, Swami Mukundananda, Jay Shetty, Simon Sinek, Ankur Warikoo and Jeff Keller.

Visit our Website

Boasting one of India's largest book distribution networks, Jaico has its headquarters in Mumbai, with branches in Ahmedabad, Bangalore, Chennai, Delhi, Hyderabad, and Kolkata. This network ensures that our books reach all parts of the country, both urban and rural.